Video Basics 5 Workbook

Herbert Zettl

San Francisco State University

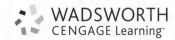

WADSWORTH
CENGAGE Learning™

Australia • Brazil • Japan • Korea • Mexico • Singapore • Spain • United Kingdom • United States

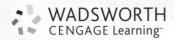

Video Basics Workbook, Fifth Edition
Herbert Zettl

Publisher: Holly J. Allen

Senior Development Editor: Renee Deljon

Assistant Editor: Lucinda Bingham

Editorial Assistant: Meghan Bass

Technology Project Manager: Jeanette Wiseman

Managing Marketing Manager: Kimberly Russell

Marketing Assistant: Alexandra Tran

Senior Marketing Communications Manager:
    Shemika Britt

Project Manager, Editorial Production:
    Catherine Morris

Creative Director: Rob Hugel

Art Director: Maria Epes

Print Buyer: Judy Inouye

Permissions Editor: Bob Kauser

Production Service: Ideas to Images

Compositor: Ideas to Images

Art Editor: Gary Palmatier

Photo Researcher: Cheri Throop

Copy Editor: Elizabeth von Radics

Illustrator: Ideas to Images

Text and Cover Designer: Gary Palmatier,
    Ideas to Images

Cover Images: Alex Zettl and Sony Electronics, Inc.

For product information and technology assistance, contact us at **Cengage Learning Customer & Sales Support, 1-800-354-9706**

For permission to use material from this text or product, submit all requests online at **www.cengage.com/permissions** Further permissions questions can be emailed to **permissionrequest@cengage.com**

ISBN-13: 978-0-495-09269-8
ISBN-10: 0-495-09269-X

Wadsworth
25 Thomson Place
Boston, MA 02210
USA

Cengage Learning is a leading provider of customized learning solutions with office locations around the globe, including Singapore, the United Kingdom, Australia, Mexico, Brazil and Japan. Locate your local office at: international.cengage.com/region

Cengage Learning products are represented in Canada by Nelson Education, Ltd.

For your course and learning solutions, visit **academic.cengage.com**

Purchase any of our products at your local college store or at our preferred online store **www.ichapters.com**

Printed in the United States of America
2 3 4 5 6 7   11 10 09 08

Contents

Part III Image Creation: Sound, Light, Graphics, and Effects 59

Part VI Production Control: Talent and Directing 155

Photo Credits

Edward Aiona: All photos not otherwise credited

The Grass Valley Group: 94 (top), 95 (top), 103, 104, 105 (top), 106 (top), 107

Lowel-Light Mfg., Inc.: 82 (nos. 63, 67, 68)

Mole-Richardson Co.: 82 (nos. 60, 62, 65, 66)

Selco Products Company: 69 (ex. 5)

Herbert Zettl: 51 (ex. 3d), 53 (ex. 1a, 1c), 56 (ex. 6, 7), 82 (nos. 61, 64), 96 (no. 27), 143, 180 (ex. 1b)

Preface

Purpose   The primary objective of the *Video Basics 5 Workbook* is to reinforce students' learning and help them bridge, as much as possible, the gap between reading and doing. It is also intended as a convenient diagnostic tool—to find out not so much what students know but what they *don't* know. This way the instructor can spotlight certain production areas that need attention and assign appropriate field and studio production activities to make up for the deficiencies. The *Workbook* also provides the instructor with an objective tool for assessing student comprehension of the language of video production, the basic production techniques, and how to apply certain techniques in a variety of production contexts.

Organization   This edition of the *Workbook* closely follows the chapter sequence of the *Video Basics 5* text. As in the main text, the special characteristics and production requirements of digital television are emphasized throughout the *Workbook*. Despite this close correlation, however, the *Workbook* chapters are self-contained and can be assigned independently and in any order desired.

Learning objectives   All of the problems in the *Workbook* are structured with these specific learning objectives in mind:

▶ *To reinforce the learning of video terminology, production tools, and production procedures and techniques.* The review of key terms and the multiple-choice questions are to test students' knowledge of the terminology and the basic tools of video production—what they are and how they work. These exercises are to check student comprehension. If students have no trouble matching the key terms with their definitions and can answer the multiple-choice questions with relative ease without having to look up the answers in *Video Basics 5*, they have successfully learned the required material.

▶ *To facilitate the retrieval of information when needed.* By completing the review sections (except the Problem-solving Applications) without looking up any answers, students will quickly discover their strong and weak points. After pinpointing their strengths and weaknesses, they can go back to the text and, if available, to *Zettl's VideoLab 3.0* DVD-ROM and remedy their deficiencies.

▶ *To facilitate the efficient and effective application of video production equipment and practices.* The multiple-choice questions test students on what they should do—and how to do it—in various production situations. The Try It and Quiz sections of *Zettl's VideoLab 3.0* DVD-ROM offer students further opportunities to practice similar applications.

▶ *To find creative solutions to production problems.* The Problem-solving Applications challenge students to come up with creative solutions to common production problems. Note that the problem-solving section invites various answers, depending on the specific production context or available equipment. In solving these problems, students should, at least initially, not feel limited by budget and time restrictions. The floor plan and storyboard sheets are included to facilitate some of the *Workbook* problems and for students' own video productions that are independent of the *Video Basics* text requirements.

Acknowledgments   Once again, my first thanks go to the people at Wadsworth who insisted on a workbook that is as efficient in its use as it is effective in student learning. My thanks go also to Gary Palmatier of Ideas and Images for his transparent layout and clear illustrations. In concert with Elizabeth von Radics's precise editing, they eliminated possible ambiguities and greatly assist students in achieving the learning objectives.

I am also indebted to my colleagues at San Francisco State University and other institutions and especially to my students, who helped me directly or indirectly by asking questions, by making mistakes I expected, and by finding solutions I did not expect. Special thanks go to my wife, Erika, who as a longtime classroom teacher, administrator, and educational consultant once again helped me choose effective problems and objectify the answers without impinging on students' creativity.

Herbert Zettl

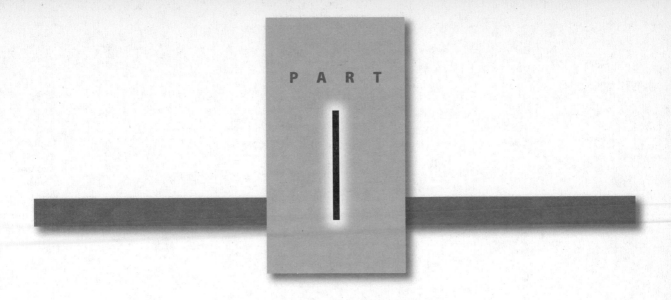

Production:
Processes and People

Course No. _____   Date _____   Name _____

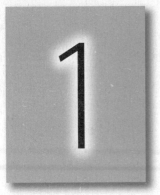 # The Production Process

REVIEW OF KEY TERMS

Match each term with its appropriate definition by filling in the corresponding bubble.

1. program objective
2. medium requirements
3. single-camera production
4. preproduction
5. production
6. multicamera production
7. postproduction
8. angle

A. Activities during which the production is telecast live or recorded.

A ○ ○ ○ ○
   1 2 3 4
   ○ ○ ○ ○
   5 6 7 8

B. The basic point of view that dominates the approach to a story.

B ○ ○ ○ ○
   1 2 3 4
   ○ ○ ○ ○
   5 6 7 8

C. The equipment, facilities, and people necessary for a specific production.

C ○ ○ ○ ○
   1 2 3 4
   ○ ○ ○ ○
   5 6 7 8

D. The effect of a program on the audience as defined in preproduction.

D ○ ○ ○ ○
   1 2 3 4
   ○ ○ ○ ○
   5 6 7 8

© 2007 Thomson Wadsworth

PAGE TOTAL [   ]

Chapter 1 — *The Production Process*

3

1. program objective	4. preproduction	7. postproduction
2. medium requirements	5. production	8. angle
3. single-camera production	6. multicamera production	

E. A film-style approach to video capture.

E ○ ○ ○ ○
  1 2 3 4
○ ○ ○ ○
5 6 7 8

F. The use of several cameras for simultaneous video capture of an event.

F ○ ○ ○ ○
  1 2 3 4
○ ○ ○ ○
5 6 7 8

G. Activities during the planning of a production.

G ○ ○ ○ ○
  1 2 3 4
○ ○ ○ ○
5 6 7 8

H. Production activities after the capturing phase.

H ○ ○ ○ ○
  1 2 3 4
○ ○ ○ ○
5 6 7 8

PAGE TOTAL ☐

SECTION TOTAL ☐

REVIEW OF PRODUCTION MODEL

1. Identify each part of the production model diagram and fill in the bubbles with the corresponding numbers.

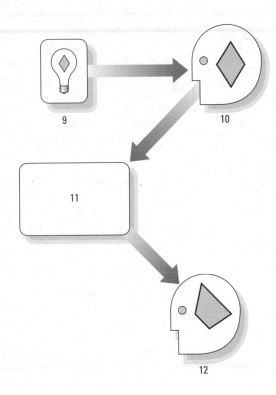

a. desired effect

b. basic idea

c. message actually received

d. medium requirements

1a ◯ ◯ ◯ ◯
   9 10 11 12

1b ◯ ◯ ◯ ◯
   9 10 11 12

1c ◯ ◯ ◯ ◯
   9 10 11 12

1d ◯ ◯ ◯ ◯
   9 10 11 12

P A G E
T O T A L [ ]

Select the correct answers and fill in the bubbles with the corresponding numbers.

2. The message that ultimately counts is the one that is (13) *carefully constructed by the producer* (14) *transmitted by the originating institution* (15) *received and interpreted by the viewer.*

| 2 | ○ 13 | ○ 14 | ○ 15 |

3. The medium requirements include (16) *equipment but not program content and people* (17) *equipment and people* (18) *equipment, production elements, and people.*

| 3 | ○ 16 | ○ 17 | ○ 18 |

4. The "angle" describes (19) *a critical view of the program objective* (20) *the basic approach to the production* (21) *the point of view of the audience.*

| 4 | ○ 19 | ○ 20 | ○ 21 |

5. The most important initial step in the production model is to (22) *determine the available production equipment* (23) *define the program objective* (24) *contact production personnel.*

| 5 | ○ 22 | ○ 23 | ○ 24 |

6. Medium requirements are basically determined by (25) *the program objective* (26) *the chief engineer* (27) *the available equipment.*

| 6 | ○ 25 | ○ 26 | ○ 27 |

7. The closer the actually received message is to the (28) *program objective* (29) *producer's objective* (30) *medium requirements,* the more successful the program.

| 7 | ○ 28 | ○ 29 | ○ 30 |

PAGE TOTAL

SECTION TOTAL

REVIEW OF SINGLE-CAMERA AND MULTICAMERA SETUPS

1. Fill in the bubbles whose numbers correspond with the appropriate camera setup as shown in the diagrams below:

a. single-camera film-style

b. multicamera switched

c. multicamera iso

1a	◯ 31	◯ 32	◯ 33
1b	◯ 31	◯ 32	◯ 33
1c	◯ 31	◯ 32	◯ 33

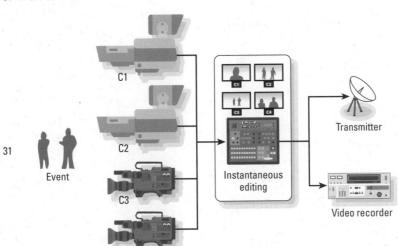

SECTION TOTAL ☐

REVIEW OF PRODUCTION PROCESSES

Select the correct answers and fill in the bubbles with the corresponding numbers.

1. In the preproduction flowchart below, match each major step with the corresponding number.

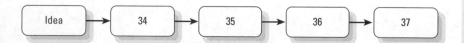

a. script

b. angle

c. evaluation

d. program objective

1a ○ ○ ○ ○
   34   35   36   37

1b ○ ○ ○ ○
   34   35   36   37

1c ○ ○ ○ ○
   34   35   36   37

1d ○ ○ ○ ○
   34   35   36   37

P A G E
T O T A L

2. In the preproduction flowchart below, match each major step with the corresponding number.

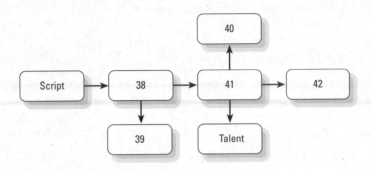

a. producer

b. art director

c. director

d. budget

e. facilities/equipment/tech personnel

2a ○ ○ ○ ○ ○
    38 39 40 41 42

2b ○ ○ ○ ○ ○
    38 39 40 41 42

2c ○ ○ ○ ○ ○
    38 39 40 41 42

2d ○ ○ ○ ○ ○
    38 39 40 41 42

2e ○ ○ ○ ○ ○
    38 39 40 41 42

P A G E
T O T A L [ ]

SECTION
TOTAL [ ]

REVIEW QUIZ

Mark the following statements as true or false by filling in the bubbles in the
T *(for true) or* ***F*** *(for false) column.*

		T	F
1.	A precise description of a specific target audience should be based on demographic as well as psychographic data.	**1** ○ 43	○ 44
2.	In the context of preproduction, an "angle" means a specific camera field of view.	**2** ○ 45	○ 46
3.	Clustering and brainstorming are similar idea-creating techniques.	**3** ○ 47	○ 48
4.	Medium requirements include production personnel, equipment, and facilities.	**4** ○ 49	○ 50
5.	The preproduction process includes the statement of the medium requirements.	**5** ○ 51	○ 52
6.	The audience is largely irrelevant when establishing the program objective.	**6** ○ 53	○ 54
7.	The program objective is important for the preproduction phase and the production phase but not the postproduction phase.	**7** ○ 55	○ 56
8.	When brainstorming for new ideas, somebody should make sure that the ideas generated are always relevant to the topic.	**8** ○ 57	○ 58
9.	The output of a multicamera setup can be fed into the switcher or into separate recorders for each camera.	**9** ○ 59	○ 60
10.	Because production is primarily a creative activity, any type of production system would prove counterproductive.	**10** ○ 61	○ 62

SECTION
TOTAL [   ]

PROBLEM-SOLVING APPLICATIONS

1. Do a brainstorming session. Have several people engaged in the same production problem sit in a circle, then place the mic of a small audiotape recorder in the center of the circle. Describe the general theme of the production, such as "improving education in this country" or "the importance of art in elementary schools." Do not try to state the general idea as a program objective. The specific program objective should develop out of the brainstorming session.

   A good way to begin is to have one of the group members say something neutral, such as "Knock-knock-who's there?" or "Hello, what can I do for you?" Make sure that *all* ideas are accepted and not commented on, however far-out or ridiculous they may be. During the playback you can be more discriminating and select only those ideas that fit your overall production theme. See whether, and how, this material might help you design a program objective and/or the medium translation of the objective.

2. Select a key word signifying your program theme and do an idea cluster. Use the cluster to develop the program objective, the specific program type (interview, documentary, drama), and the production approach (studio, ENG, EFP, single-camera, multicamera).

3. Expand the three clusters indicated in the following three figures and develop a precise program objective from each.

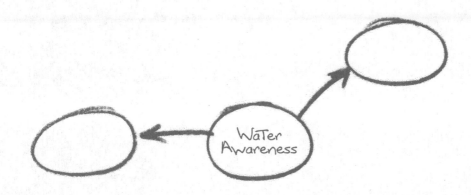

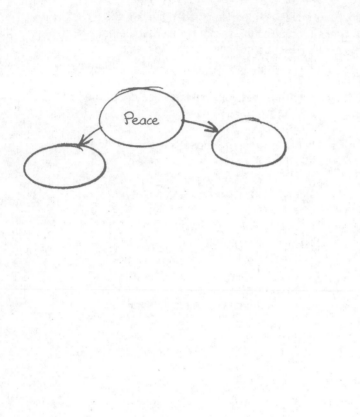

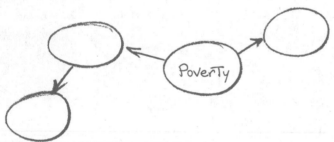

Part I — *Production: Processes and People*

2 The Production Team: Who Does What When?

REVIEW OF KEY TERMS

Match each term with its appropriate definition by filling in the corresponding bubble.

1. above-the-line
2. below-the-line
3. production schedule
4. preproduction team
5. production team
6. EFP team
7. time line
8. postproduction team

A. Consists of director, video editor, and sound designer.

A ○ ○ ○ ○
   1 2 3 4
  ○ ○ ○ ○
   5 6 7 8

B. A schedule that shows the time allotment for various activities during the production day.

B ○ ○ ○ ○
   1 2 3 4
  ○ ○ ○ ○
   5 6 7 8

C. Consists of a variety of nontechnical and technical people, such as the producer and various assistants (associate producer and PA), the director and assistant (AD), and the talent and production crew.

C ○ ○ ○ ○
   1 2 3 4
  ○ ○ ○ ○
   5 6 7 8

D. Category for technical personnel, including such crew members as camera operators, floor persons, and audio engineers.

D ○ ○ ○ ○
   1 2 3 4
  ○ ○ ○ ○
   5 6 7 8

E. Consists of people who plan the production. This team normally includes the producer, director, writer, art director, and technical supervisor or technical director (TD). Large productions may also include a composer and a choreographer.

E ○ ○ ○ ○
   1 2 3 4
  ○ ○ ○ ○
   5 6 7 8

PAGE TOTAL [ ]

1. above-the-line
2. below-the-line
3. production schedule
4. preproduction team
5. production team
6. EFP team
7. time line
8. postproduction team

F. Usually the talent, camcorder operator, and utility person.

F ○ ○ ○ ○
  1 2 3 4
  ○ ○ ○ ○
  5 6 7 8

G. Category for nontechnical personnel, such as producers, directors, and talent.

G ○ ○ ○ ○
  1 2 3 4
  ○ ○ ○ ○
  5 6 7 8

H. A calendar that lists major production activities.

H ○ ○ ○ ○
  1 2 3 4
  ○ ○ ○ ○
  5 6 7 8

PAGE TOTAL

SECTION TOTAL

REVIEW OF PRODUCTION PERSONNEL AND RESPONSIBILITIES

Identify the production person mainly responsible for the following production situations and fill in the bubbles with the corresponding numbers.

1. To increase the overall light level in a scene, you should ask the (9) *LD* (10) *PA* (11) *floor manager.*

   1 ◯ 9   ◯ 10   ◯ 11

2. Making sure that the dancers can hear the music tape is the responsibility of the (12) *LD* (13) *AD* (14) *audio engineer.*

   2 ◯ 12   ◯ 13   ◯ 14

3. The talent wants to make sure that he can see the opening cues. He should talk to the (15) *director* (16) *producer* (17) *floor manager.*

   3 ◯ 15   ◯ 16   ◯ 17

4. Informing talent and crew about a videotaping schedule change is the responsibility of the (18) *floor manager* (19) *producer* (20) *TD.*

   4 ◯ 18   ◯ 19   ◯ 20

5. The producer complains about the "static look" of the show. To correct the situation, she must talk to the (21) *TD* (22) *art director* (23) *executive producer.*

   5 ◯ 21   ◯ 22   ◯ 23

6. The person in charge of camera rehearsals is the (24) *director* (25) *AD* (26) *TD.*

   6 ◯ 24   ◯ 25   ◯ 26

7. Having the scenery set up and the set decorated by the scheduled time is the responsibility of the (27) *floor manager* (28) *director* (29) *TD.*

   7 ◯ 27   ◯ 28   ◯ 29

8. The time line is done by the (30) *floor manager* (31) *director* (32) *art director.*

   8 ◯ 30   ◯ 31   ◯ 32

9. Last-minute changes to the names on the final credits are made by the (33) *art director* (34) *TD* (35) *C.G. operator.*

   9 ◯ 33   ◯ 34   ◯ 35

10. Arranging various shots in postproduction is done by the (36) *producer* (37) *video operator* (38) *editor.*

    10 ◯ 36   ◯ 37   ◯ 38

SECTION TOTAL ☐

REVIEW OF THE TIME LINE

From the list below, select the major items omitted from the following time line and fill in the corresponding bubbles. Note: This list contains items that are not part of the customary time line.

Production Schedule: April 15—Panel Discussion (Studio 1)

8:30–9:00 a.m.	Tech meeting
9:00–11:00 a.m.	Setup and lighting
12:00–12:15 p.m.	Notes and reset
12:15–12:30 p.m.	Briefing of panel guests
12:30–12:45 p.m.	Run-through and camera rehearsal
12:45–12:55 p.m.	Notes and reset
12:55–2:55 p.m.	Taping
2:55–3:30 p.m.	Spill

(39) *tech meeting*

(40) *taping*

(41) *crew call*

(42) *notes*

(43) *strike*

(44) *camera rehearsal*

(45) *break*

(46) *lighting*

(47) *reset*

(48) *meal*

(49) *budget meeting*

(50) *preproduction meeting*

○ ○ ○ ○
39 40 41 42

○ ○ ○ ○
43 44 45 46

○ ○ ○ ○
47 48 49 50

SECTION
TOTAL

REVIEW QUIZ

Mark the following statements as true or false by filling in the bubbles in the
T *(for true) or* ***F*** *(for false) column.*

		T	F
1.	The director should have some influence on postproduction editing.	1 ○ 51	○ 52
2.	The LD is in charge of directing the log entries.	2 ○ 53	○ 54
3.	Talent includes actors but not performers.	3 ○ 55	○ 56
4.	The audio engineer works the audio console during a show.	4 ○ 57	○ 58
5.	The PA is usually responsible for notes.	5 ○ 59	○ 60
6.	The executive producer is always part of the field survey team.	6 ○ 61	○ 62
7.	Principal camera positions and talent blocking are determined by the director.	7 ○ 63	○ 64
8.	Normally, the TD runs the video recorder.	8 ○ 65	○ 66
9.	The art director is responsible for putting up the studio set.	9 ○ 67	○ 68
10.	The AD is involved in preproduction but not production.	10 ○ 69	○ 70
11.	The editor is part of the preproduction team.	11 ○ 71	○ 72
12.	The floor manager is principally responsible for the budget.	12 ○ 73	○ 74

SECTION
TOTAL [   ]

PROBLEM-SOLVING APPLICATIONS

1. The camera operators for a weekly two-camera interview series tell you, the producer, that they do not need a director because they have done the show many times and know every shot by heart. Do you agree? If so, why? If not, why not?

2. The ENG/EFP camcorder operator of a weekly on-location interview show tells you, the producer, that he does not need a director because he has done the show many times and knows what shots are required. Do you agree? If so, why? If not, why not?

3. The director of video production in a large high-tech company tells you that she has agreed to pay specific fees for the above-the-line personnel but a lump sum for all below-the-line costs. What does she mean?

4. The PA complains that the producer, the director, and even the floor manager ask her to write down specific production problems. Her comment is that, as a production assistant, she has to listen only to the producer. Is her complaint justified?

5. The talent complains to the director about the long hours and the relatively low pay. Is the talent complaining to the right person? If so, why? If not, to whom should the talent direct the complaints?

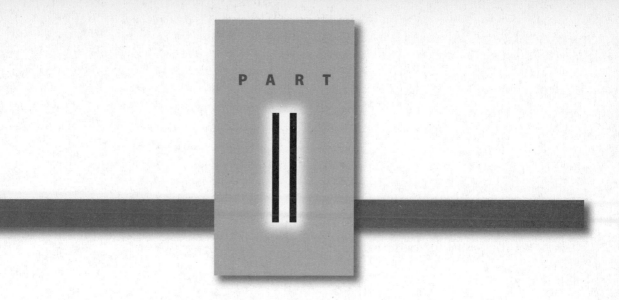

Image Creation:
Digital Video and Camera

3 Image Formation and Digital Video

REVIEW OF KEY TERMS

Match each term with its appropriate definition by filling in the corresponding bubble.

1. **720p**
2. **1080i**
3. **analog**
4. **digital**
5. **compression**

6. **sampling**
7. **RGB**
8. **HDV**
9. **HDTV**
10. **interlaced scanning**

11. **progressive scanning**
12. **field**
13. **frame**
14. **quantizing**
15. **refresh rate**

A. A step in the digitizing of an analog signal. It changes the sampling points into discrete values.

A
○ ○ ○ ○ ○
1 2 3 4 5
○ ○ ○ ○ ○
6 7 8 9 10
○ ○ ○ ○ ○
11 12 13 14 15

B. A signal that fluctuates exactly like the original stimulus.

B
○ ○ ○ ○ ○
1 2 3 4 5
○ ○ ○ ○ ○
6 7 8 9 10
○ ○ ○ ○ ○
11 12 13 14 15

C. A complete scanning cycle of the electron beam, consisting of two fields.

C
○ ○ ○ ○ ○
1 2 3 4 5
○ ○ ○ ○ ○
6 7 8 9 10
○ ○ ○ ○ ○
11 12 13 14 15

D. The scanning cycle of all odd or even lines.

D
○ ○ ○ ○ ○
1 2 3 4 5
○ ○ ○ ○ ○
6 7 8 9 10
○ ○ ○ ○ ○
11 12 13 14 15

PAGE TOTAL ☐

© 2007 Thomson Wadsworth

1. 720p	6. sampling	11. progressive scanning
2. 1080i	7. RGB	12. field
3. analog	8. HDV	13. frame
4. digital	9. HDTV	14. quantizing
5. compression	10. interlaced scanning	15. refresh rate

E. The system that scans all odd-numbered lines and then all even-numbered lines.

E
○ ○ ○ ○ ○
1　2　3　4　5
○ ○ ○ ○ ○
6　7　8　9　10
○ ○ ○ ○ ○
11　12　13　14　15

F. Selecting a great number of small parts of the analog signal at equally spaced intervals.

F
○ ○ ○ ○ ○
1　2　3　4　5
○ ○ ○ ○ ○
6　7　8　9　10
○ ○ ○ ○ ○
11　12　13　14　15

G. A recording system that produces the same resolution as HDTV but which is more compressed than HDTV.

G
○ ○ ○ ○ ○
1　2　3　4　5
○ ○ ○ ○ ○
6　7　8　9　10
○ ○ ○ ○ ○
11　12　13　14　15

H. High-definition television.

H
○ ○ ○ ○ ○
1　2　3　4　5
○ ○ ○ ○ ○
6　7　8　9　10
○ ○ ○ ○ ○
11　12　13　14　15

I. The basic colors of television.

I
○ ○ ○ ○ ○
1　2　3　4　5
○ ○ ○ ○ ○
6　7　8　9　10
○ ○ ○ ○ ○
11　12　13　14　15

J. The scanning system that consists of two 540-line fields. (Some claim that there are two 539½-line fields.)

J
○ ○ ○ ○ ○
1　2　3　4　5
○ ○ ○ ○ ○
6　7　8　9　10
○ ○ ○ ○ ○
11　12　13　14　15

PAGE
TOTAL [ ]

1. 720p	6. sampling	11. progressive scanning
2. 1080i	7. RGB	12. field
3. analog	8. HDV	13. frame
4. digital	9. HDTV	14. quantizing
5. compression	10. interlaced scanning	15. refresh rate

K. The temporary rearrangement or elimination of redundant picture information for more-efficient storage and signal transport.

K
○ ○ ○ ○ ○
1 2 3 4 5
○ ○ ○ ○ ○
6 7 8 9 10
○ ○ ○ ○ ○
11 12 13 14 15

L. The number of complete scanning cycles per second.

L
○ ○ ○ ○ ○
1 2 3 4 5
○ ○ ○ ○ ○
6 7 8 9 10
○ ○ ○ ○ ○
11 12 13 14 15

M. One of the accepted progressive scanning systems of DTV.

M
○ ○ ○ ○ ○
1 2 3 4 5
○ ○ ○ ○ ○
6 7 8 9 10
○ ○ ○ ○ ○
11 12 13 14 15

N. Data in an on/off configuration.

N
○ ○ ○ ○ ○
1 2 3 4 5
○ ○ ○ ○ ○
6 7 8 9 10
○ ○ ○ ○ ○
11 12 13 14 15

O. The consecutive scanning from top to bottom.

O
○ ○ ○ ○ ○
1 2 3 4 5
○ ○ ○ ○ ○
6 7 8 9 10
○ ○ ○ ○ ○
11 12 13 14 15

PAGE TOTAL [ ]

SECTION TOTAL [ ]

REVIEW OF BASIC IMAGE FORMATION

Select the correct answers and fill in the bubbles with the corresponding numbers.

1. An interlaced frame of standard NTSC television consists of (16) *four fields*
    (17) *two fields* (18) *three fields.*

    1 ◯ 16 ◯ 17 ◯ 18

2. The scanning of a single field takes (19) *½₀ second* (20) *⅓₀ second*
    (21) *¹⁄₆₀ second.*

    2 ◯ 19 ◯ 20 ◯ 21

3. The scanning of a complete interlaced NTSC frame takes (22) *½₀ second*
    (23) *⅓₀ second* (24) *¹⁄₆₀ second.*

    3 ◯ 22 ◯ 23 ◯ 24

4. In progressive scanning each scanning cycle produces a (25) *field* (26) *frame.*

    4 ◯ 25 ◯ 26

5. In progressive scanning (27) *only the odd-numbered lines are scanned*
    (28) *only the even-numbered lines are scanned* (29) *each line is scanned from
    top to bottom in sequence.*

    5 ◯ 27 ◯ 28 ◯ 29

6. HDTV can use (30) *only interlaced scanning* (31) *only progressive scanning*
    (32) *either of the two.*

    6 ◯ 30 ◯ 31 ◯ 32

7. To produce a color image, a standard television receiver needs (33) *one*
    (34) *two* (35) *three* electron beams.

    7 ◯ 33 ◯ 34 ◯ 35

8. Each scanning line is made up of (36) *pixels* (37) *digits* (38) *numbers.*

    8 ◯ 36 ◯ 37 ◯ 38

SECTION TOTAL [   ]

REVIEW OF ANALOG AND DIGITAL PROCESSES

Select the correct answers and fill in the bubbles with the corresponding numbers.

1. A digital signal operates on the (39) *on/off* (40) *continuous wave* (41) *sine wave* principle.

2. The binary on/off code is normally represented by (42) *0's and 1's* (43) *1's and 2's* (44) *0's and 00's.*

3. One of the chief advantages of a digital over an analog video signal is that the digital signal (45) *can be dubbed many times without noticeable deterioration* (46) *can be sampled* (47) *can be interlaced.*

4. The compression system that eliminates redundant digital information is called (48) *low-sampling* (49) *lossy* (50) *high-sampling.*

5. In the digitizing process, the sampling rate should be (51) *as high as possible* (52) *as low as possible* (53) *neither because sampling is not a digitizing step.*

6. Which of the two sampling rates shown below will produce the higher-quality signal?

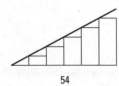

54

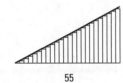

55

7. The compression systems that compares frames for redundant information is called (56) *JPEG-3* (57) *MPEG-2* (58) *CODEC-4.*

1	○ 39	○ 40	○ 41
2	○ 42	○ 43	○ 44
3	○ 45	○ 46	○ 47
4	○ 48	○ 49	○ 50
5	○ 51	○ 52	○ 53
6	○ 54	○ 55	
7	○ 56	○ 57	○ 58

SECTION TOTAL ☐

*Mark the following statements as true or false by filling in the bubbles in the **T** (for true) or **F** (for false) column.*

		T	F
1.	A black-and-white image on a color set is created by a "black" electron gun.	1 ○ 59	○ 60
2.	In progressive scanning, each line is scanned consecutively from top to bottom.	2 ○ 61	○ 62
3.	In progressive scanning, each scanning cycle from top to bottom generates a field.	3 ○ 63	○ 64
4.	In interlaced scanning, each scanning cycle from top to bottom generates a frame.	4 ○ 65	○ 66
5.	MPEG-2 is a lossy compression system.	5 ○ 67	○ 68
6.	In progressive scanning, four fields make up a complete frame	6 ○ 69	○ 70
7.	Lossy compression is rarely used because it always leads to noticeable picture deterioration.	7 ○ 71	○ 72
8.	HDV is identical to HDTV.	8 ○ 73	○ 74
9.	The 720p scanning system produces 30 interlaced frames per second.	9 ○ 75	○ 76
10.	In interlaced scanning, two fields make up a complete frame.	10 ○ 77	○ 78
11.	Similar to digital signals, analog signals can have lossy or lossless states of compression.	11 ○ 79	○ 80
12.	The digital signal fluctuates exactly like the original stimulus.	12 ○ 81	○ 82
13.	A digital signal can be compressed with various codecs.	13 ○ 83	○ 84
14.	An analog signal can be compressed with MPEG-2 as well as JPEG codecs.	14 ○ 85	○ 86
15.	In a digital system, the *on* state is usually represented by a 1, the *off* state by a 0.	15 ○ 87	○ 88

SECTION TOTAL [ ]

PROBLEM-SOLVING APPLICATIONS

1. You are asked to explain why, in most cases, we prefer digital over analog systems in video production. What is your response?

2. Demonstrate the relationship of sampling rate to signal fidelity. What graphics would you use? Why?

3. You are asked to explain the basic difference between interlaced and progressive scanning. What are the advantages and the disadvantages of each system?

4. Why do we have different codecs, and what are their functions?

4 The Video Camera

REVIEW OF KEY TERMS

Match each term with its appropriate definition by filling in the corresponding bubble.

1. camera chain
2. camcorder
3. CCD
4. ENG/EFP camera
5. HDTV camera
6. fast lens
7. pixel
8. aperture
9. focal length
10. zoom range
11. *f*-stop
12. beam splitter

A. The iris opening of a lens.

A ○ ○ ○ ○
   1 2 3 4
○ ○ ○ ○
5 6 7 8
○ ○ ○ ○
9 10 11 12

B. A lens that permits a relatively great amount of light to pass through at its largest aperture setting.

B ○ ○ ○ ○
   1 2 3 4
○ ○ ○ ○
5 6 7 8
○ ○ ○ ○
9 10 11 12

C. The camera connected with the CCU, power supply, and sync generator.

C ○ ○ ○ ○
   1 2 3 4
○ ○ ○ ○
5 6 7 8
○ ○ ○ ○
9 10 11 12

D. An electronic "chip." It is the most common imaging device in color cameras.

D ○ ○ ○ ○
   1 2 3 4
○ ○ ○ ○
5 6 7 8
○ ○ ○ ○
9 10 11 12

PAGE
TOTAL

1. camera chain	5. HDTV camera	9. focal length
2. camcorder	6. fast lens	10. zoom range
3. CCD	7. pixel	11. *f*-stop
4. ENG/EFP camera	8. aperture	12. beam splitter

E. Picture element.

E
○ ○ ○ ○
1 2 3 4
○ ○ ○ ○
5 6 7 8
○ ○ ○ ○
9 10 11 12

F. The calibration on the lens indicating the aperture (and therefore the amount of light passing through the lens).

F
○ ○ ○ ○
1 2 3 4
○ ○ ○ ○
5 6 7 8
○ ○ ○ ○
9 10 11 12

G. A portable camera with the VTR attached to it to form a single, independent unit.

G
○ ○ ○ ○
1 2 3 4
○ ○ ○ ○
5 6 7 8
○ ○ ○ ○
9 10 11 12

H. A high-resolution camera.

H
○ ○ ○ ○
1 2 3 4
○ ○ ○ ○
5 6 7 8
○ ○ ○ ○
9 10 11 12

I. The degree to which the focal length can be changed from a wide shot to a close-up during a zoom.

I
○ ○ ○ ○
1 2 3 4
○ ○ ○ ○
5 6 7 8
○ ○ ○ ○
9 10 11 12

J. A portable camera, without a built-in VTR, that contains all camera controls in the camera itself.

J
○ ○ ○ ○
1 2 3 4
○ ○ ○ ○
5 6 7 8
○ ○ ○ ○
9 10 11 12

PAGE
TOTAL

1. camera chain	5. HDTV camera	9. focal length
2. camcorder	6. fast lens	10. zoom range
3. CCD	7. pixel	11. *f*-stop
4. ENG/EFP camera	8. aperture	12. beam splitter

K. Indicates how much of a scene the lens can see and how magnified the distant object looks.

K ◯ ◯ ◯ ◯
   1 2 3 4
   ◯ ◯ ◯ ◯
   5 6 7 8
   ◯ ◯ ◯ ◯
   9 10 11 12

L. Optical device within the camera that splits the white light into three primary colors: red, green, and blue.

L ◯ ◯ ◯ ◯
   1 2 3 4
   ◯ ◯ ◯ ◯
   5 6 7 8
   ◯ ◯ ◯ ◯
   9 10 11 12

PAGE TOTAL [ ]

SECTION TOTAL [ ]

REVIEW OF CAMERA
FUNCTION AND ELEMENTS

Select the correct answers and fill in the bubbles with the corresponding numbers.

1. The basic parts of the video camera are (13) *pedestal* (14) *lens* (15) *VTR* (16) *imaging device* (17) *viewfinder* (18) *tally light.* **(Fill in three bubbles.)**

1　○ 13　○ 14　○ 15
　　○ 16　○ 17　○ 18

2. Fill in the bubbles whose numbers correspond with the camera elements shown in the following figure.

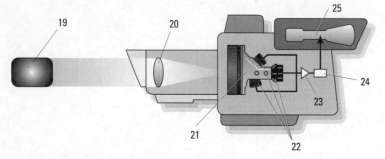

a. Transforms light into electric energy or video signals.

2a　○ 19　○ 20　○ 21　○ 22
　　○ 23　○ 24　○ 25

b. Converts video signals back into visible screen images.

2b　○ 19　○ 20　○ 21　○ 22
　　○ 23　○ 24　○ 25

c. Gathers and transmits the light.

2c　○ 19　○ 20　○ 21　○ 22
　　○ 23　○ 24　○ 25

d. Amplifies video signals.

2d　○ 19　○ 20　○ 21　○ 22
　　○ 23　○ 24　○ 25

e. Processes video signal.

2e　○ 19　○ 20　○ 21　○ 22
　　○ 23　○ 24　○ 25

f. Reflects light.

2f　○ 19　○ 20　○ 21　○ 22
　　○ 23　○ 24　○ 25

g. Splits the white light into red, green, and blue light beams.

2g　○ 19　○ 20　○ 21　○ 22
　　○ 23　○ 24　○ 25

SECTION TOTAL

REVIEW OF LENSES

Select the correct answers and fill in the bubbles with the corresponding numbers.

1. A fast lens transmits an image (26) *faster* (27) *more slowly* than a slow lens, or permits (28) *more* (29) *less* light to enter, assuming a maximum aperture. **(Fill in two bubbles.)**

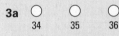

2. A zoom lens has a (30) *wide* (31) *normal* (32) *narrow* (33) *variable* focal length.

3. In the diagram below, select the most appropriate *f*-stop number for each of the four apertures (a through d) and fill in the bubbles with the corresponding number.

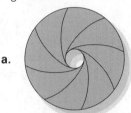

a.   (34) *f*/22   (35) *f*/5.6   (36) *f*1.4

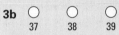

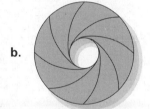

b.   (37) *f*/1.4   (38) *f*/2.8   (39) *f*/16

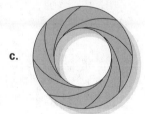

c.   (40) *f*/1.4   (41) *f*/4   (42) *f*/16

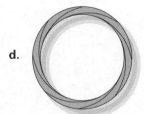

d.   (43) *f*/1.4   (44) *f*/8   (45) *f*/22

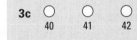

4. A short-focal-length lens gives (46) *a wider view than* (47) *a closer view than* (48) *the same vista as* a long-focal-length lens.

5. When reaching the maximum digital zoom-in position, the picture gets progressively (49) *sharper* (50) *smaller* (51) *fuzzier.*

SECTION TOTAL

REVIEW OF THE IMAGING DEVICE, SIGNAL PROCESSING, AND CAMERA CHAIN

Select the correct answers and fill in the bubbles with the corresponding numbers.

1. The more pixels a CCD imaging device contains, the (52) *sharper* (53) *brighter* (54) *more colorful* the resulting screen image will be.

2. The highest-quality images are produced by (55) *single-chip* (56) *two-chip* (57) *three-chip* cameras.

3. The NTSC signal is a (58) *composite* (59) *component* (60) *complex* signal.

4. The luminance signal is a (61) *color* (62) *composite* (63) *black-and-white* signal.

5. Camcorders do not need a (64) *power supply* (65) *video recorder* (66) *cable that connects them to the VTR.*

6. The standard studio camera chain consists of (67) *power supply, sync generator, and CCD* (68) *camera head, power supply, sync generator, and CCU* (69) *CCU, CCD, and power supply.*

7. The beam splitter changes (70) *the incoming light into RGB light beams* (71) *the incoming light into an electrical signal* (72) *the incoming light into color and black-and-white signals.*

8. The STV NTSC signal (73) *keeps the Y and C signals separate throughout signal transport and recording* (74) *combines the Y and C signals only during the recording process* (75) *combines the Y and C signals during transport and recording.*

9. Studio cameras are normally controlled by (76) *their internal auto controls* (77) *an external CCU* (78) *an internal CCU.*

10. Electronic cinema cameras use as recording media (79) *16mm film* (80) *35mm film* (81) *videotape.*

#			
1	◯ 52	◯ 53	◯ 54
2	◯ 55	◯ 56	◯ 57
3	◯ 58	◯ 59	◯ 60
4	◯ 61	◯ 62	◯ 63
5	◯ 64	◯ 65	◯ 66
6	◯ 67	◯ 68	◯ 69
7	◯ 70	◯ 71	◯ 72
8	◯ 73	◯ 74	◯ 75
9	◯ 76	◯ 77	◯ 78
10	◯ 79	◯ 80	◯ 81

SECTION TOTAL

REVIEW QUIZ

Mark the following statements as true or false by filling in the bubbles in the **T** *(for true) or* **F** *(for false) column.*

		T	F
1.	Most HDV camcorders can record in 720p and 1080i.	1 ○ 82	○ 83
2.	A CCD translates light into electric energy.	2 ○ 84	○ 85
3.	The CCU performs camera setup and control functions but does not help with keeping in focus during a zoom.	3 ○ 86	○ 87
4.	The sync generator and the power supply fulfill similar functions.	4 ○ 88	○ 89
5.	ENG/EFP cameras are the same as ENG/EFP camcorders.	5 ○ 90	○ 91
6.	Camcorders can come with or without a video-recording device.	6 ○ 92	○ 93
7.	A beam splitter divides the incoming white light into red, green, and blue light beams.	7 ○ 94	○ 95
8.	The ENG/EFP camera contains the major parts of the regular camera chain.	8 ○ 96	○ 97
9.	The wide-angle position of the zoom lens provides a vista similar to that of a short-focal-length lens.	9 ○ 98	○ 99
10.	The lower the *f*-stop number, the larger the aperture.	10 ○ 100	○ 101
11.	ENG/EFP cameras can be connected to an RCU.	11 ○ 102	○ 103
12.	*Zoom range* refers to how fast you can zoom in or out.	12 ○ 104	○ 105
13.	All video cables must have BNC connectors.	13 ○ 106	○ 107
14.	Electronic cinema cameras are high-end HDTV camcorders.	14 ○ 108	○ 109
15.	The speed of a lens is judged by its minimum *f*-stop number.	15 ○ 110	○ 111

SECTION TOTAL [   ]

PROBLEM-SOLVING APPLICATIONS

1. The camera operator tells you not to worry about the bright white cap of the dark-skinned golf pro. He says that the automatic iris of the camcorder will take care of the proper exposure. What is your reaction?

2. The director of a multicamera field production is worried that the cameras might not deliver pictures whose colors match when edited together. The TD tells the director that the use of RCUs will greatly help in color matching. Do you agree with the TD?

3. The director tells you that for covering an outdoor sporting event, a lens with a great zoom range is more important than an extremely fast one. Why does the director think so?

4. The director of a multicamera studio show is worried about having one of the cameras pan from a very brightly lighted scene to a very dark one. The TD tells her not to worry because the VO will use the CCU to take care of such problems. Why was the director worried about this pan in the first place? What was the TD talking about, and do you agree with the TD?

5 Operating the Camera

REVIEW OF KEY TERMS

Match each term with its appropriate definition by filling in the corresponding bubble.

1. arc
2. dolly
3. cant
4. crane
5. truck

6. tongue
7. mounting head
8. tilt
9. pedestal
10. pan

11. white balance
12. calibrate zoom lens
13. shutter speed
14. jib arm

A. Small crane that can be operated by the camera operator.

A
○ ○ ○ ○ ○
1 2 3 4 5
○ ○ ○ ○ ○
6 7 8 9 10
○ ○ ○ ○
11 12 13 14

B. To move the camera in a slightly curved dolly or truck.

B
○ ○ ○ ○ ○
1 2 3 4 5
○ ○ ○ ○ ○
6 7 8 9 10
○ ○ ○ ○
11 12 13 14

C. A device that connects the camera to its support.

C
○ ○ ○ ○ ○
1 2 3 4 5
○ ○ ○ ○ ○
6 7 8 9 10
○ ○ ○ ○
11 12 13 14

D. To move the boom with the camera from left to right or from right to left.

D
○ ○ ○ ○ ○
1 2 3 4 5
○ ○ ○ ○ ○
6 7 8 9 10
○ ○ ○ ○
11 12 13 14

PAGE
TOTAL [   ]

1. arc	6. tongue	11. white balance
2. dolly	7. mounting head	12. calibrate zoom lens
3. cant	8. tilt	13. shutter speed
4. crane	9. pedestal	14. jib arm
5. truck	10. pan	

E. To point the camera up or down.

E
1 2 3 4 5
6 7 8 9 10
11 12 13 14

F. To move the camera up or down with a studio camera mount.

F
1 2 3 4 5
6 7 8 9 10
11 12 13 14

G. Horizontal turning of the camera.

G
1 2 3 4 5
6 7 8 9 10
11 12 13 14

H. To preset a zoom lens to keep it in focus throughout the zoom.

H
1 2 3 4 5
6 7 8 9 10
11 12 13 14

I. The adjustment of the color channels in the camera to produce a white color in lighting of various color temperatures.

I
1 2 3 4 5
6 7 8 9 10
11 12 13 14

J. To move the camera toward or away from the object.

J
1 2 3 4 5
6 7 8 9 10
11 12 13 14

PAGE
TOTAL

1. arc	6. tongue	11. white balance
2. dolly	7. mounting head	12. calibrate zoom lens
3. cant	8. tilt	13. shutter speed
4. crane	9. pedestal	14. jib arm
5. truck	10. pan	

K. To move the camera laterally by means of a mobile camera mount.

L. Tilting the camera sideways.

M. To move the boom of the camera crane up or down.

N. The higher it is set, the sharper a moving object will be.

K 1 2 3 4 5 6 7 8 9 10 11 12 13 14

L 1 2 3 4 5 6 7 8 9 10 11 12 13 14

M 1 2 3 4 5 6 7 8 9 10 11 12 13 14

N 1 2 3 4 5 6 7 8 9 10 11 12 13 14

PAGE TOTAL

SECTION TOTAL

REVIEW OF CAMERA MOUNTS

Select the correct answers and fill in the bubbles with the corresponding numbers.

1. A spreader (15) *keeps the tripod legs from spreading too far* (16) *helps spread the tripod legs as much as possible* (17) *maximizes the spread of the tripod legs.*

2. The quick-release plate (18) *facilitates the mounting of a camera on the mounting head* (19) *secures the dolly base to the tripod legs.*

3. Fill in the bubbles whose numbers correspond with the camera movements indicated in the following figure.

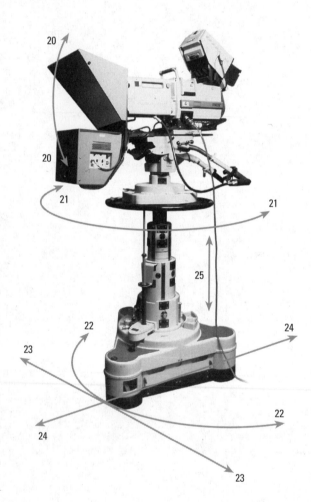

a. dolly

1 ○ ○ ○
   15 16 17

2 ○ ○
   18 19

3a ○ ○ ○
   20 21 22
   ○ ○ ○
   23 24 25

P A G E
T O T A L

b. truck

3b
○ 20 ○ 21 ○ 22
○ 23 ○ 24 ○ 25

c. tilt

3c
○ 20 ○ 21 ○ 22
○ 23 ○ 24 ○ 25

d. pan

3d
○ 20 ○ 21 ○ 22
○ 23 ○ 24 ○ 25

e. pedestal

3e
○ 20 ○ 21 ○ 22
○ 23 ○ 24 ○ 25

f. arc

3f
○ 20 ○ 21 ○ 22
○ 23 ○ 24 ○ 25

4. Identify in the following figure whether the dolly wheels on this studio pedestal are set for (26) *parallel* (27) *tricycle* or (28) *freewheeling* steering.

4
○ 26 ○ 27 ○ 28

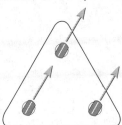

5. For all normal camera moves, the studio pedestal is normally set for (29) *parallel* (30) *tricycle* (31) *freewheeling* steering.

5
○ 29 ○ 30 ○ 31

6. To minimize the wiggles of a handheld or shoulder-mounted camcorder, you should have the camera lens (32) *zoomed out all the way (wide-angle position)* (33) *zoomed in all the way (narrow-angle position)* (34) *zoomed in halfway (normal-focal-length position)*.

6
○ 32 ○ 33 ○ 34

7. A mounting head's drag control is important (35) *only for heavy studio cameras* (36) *only for lightweight camcorders* (37) *for both studio cameras and camcorders*.

7
○ 35 ○ 36 ○ 37

P A G E
T O T A L [   ]

SECTION
T O T A L [   ]

REVIEW OF OPERATIONAL FEATURES

Select the correct answers and fill in the bubbles with the corresponding numbers.

1. Calibrating, or presetting, the zoom lens means (38) *adjusting the zoom lens so that it keeps in focus throughout the zoom* (39) *setting the proper f-stop* (40) *adjusting the zoom range.*

   1 ◯ ◯ ◯
      38 39 40

2. Proper calibration of the zoom lens requires that you (41) *zoom in* (42) *zoom out* and focus on the target object (43) *closest to* (44) *farthest from* the camera. **(Fill in two bubbles.)**

   2 ◯ ◯
      41 42
      ◯ ◯
      43 44

3. It is easiest to keep the image in focus when you are zoomed (45) *all the way in* (46) *halfway in* (47) *all the way out.*

   3 ◯ ◯ ◯
      45 46 47

4. To cant a shoulder-mounted camcorder, you must tilt it (48) *down* (49) *sideways* (50) *up.*

   4 ◯ ◯ ◯
      48 49 50

5. When white-balancing an ENG/EFP camera for covering a school board meeting in the school's multipurpose room, you should white-balance the camera (51) *in the hallway before entering the room* (52) *with a special white-balancing light* (53) *in the light that actually illuminates the area where the school board members sit.*

   5 ◯ ◯ ◯
      51 52 53

6. When a fast-moving object blurs, you need to (54) *increase the shutter speed* (55) *decrease the shutter speed* (56) *open the aperture.*

   6 ◯ ◯ ◯
      54 55 56

SECTION TOTAL [ ]

REVIEW QUIZ

Mark the following statements as true or false by filling in the bubbles in the **T** *(for true) or* **F** *(for false) column.*

		T	F
1.	Calibrating the zoom lens is necessary for ENG/EFP cameras as well as for studio cameras.	**1** ○ 57	○ 58
2.	HDV and HDTV cameras are easier to focus than standard digital camcorders.	**2** ○ 59	○ 60
3.	With a jib arm, you can boom, tongue, and pan the camera in a single motion.	**3** ○ 61	○ 62
4.	The quick-release plate ensures that the camera is mounted in an optimally balanced position when put back on the tripod or pedestal.	**4** ○ 63	○ 64
5.	The jib arm and the camera crane can make the camera move in similar ways.	**5** ○ 65	○ 66
6.	To calibrate a zoom lens, you must first zoom in and focus on the target object.	**6** ○ 67	○ 68
7.	The professional ENG/EFP camera requires new white-balancing every time the camera is moved from one lighting environment to the next.	**7** ○ 69	○ 70
8.	To tilt up means to raise the camera pedestal.	**8** ○ 71	○ 72
9.	The depth of field depends on the focal length of the lens, the lens aperture, and the distance from camera to object.	**9** ○ 73	○ 74
10.	The automatic focus on a camcorder guarantees staying in focus at all times.	**10** ○ 75	○ 76
11.	Zooming all the way in will minimize camera wobbles.	**11** ○ 77	○ 78
12.	Dolly and truck movements show up as similar movements on the screen.	**12** ○ 79	○ 80
13.	Generally, tight close-ups have a shallow depth of field.	**13** ○ 81	○ 82
14.	To avoid blurring a fast-moving object, you need to use a high shutter speed.	**14** ○ 83	○ 84
15.	The best way to lock the camera mounting head when leaving the camera unattended is to tighten the drag control.	**15** ○ 85	○ 86

SECTION TOTAL ☐

© 2007 Thomson Wadsworth

PROBLEM-SOLVING APPLICATIONS

1. Locate the tilt and pan drag and lock mechanisms of your camera. Adjust them so that you can pan and tilt the camera as smoothly as necessary. When do you need to use the lock mechanisms?

2. Place three chairs along the z-axis about 9 feet apart. Zoom in to an ECU on the first chair. It will probably be out of focus at the end of the zoom. Now bring the picture into focus. When zooming out, the picture will remain in focus. Without touching the focus, now zoom in on the last chair. Again, the picture will probably get out of focus when reaching the ECU position. Now focus on the last chair and zoom back. Without adjusting the focus, zoom in on the first chair, zoom back, and then zoom in again on the last chair. Will the first as well as the last chair remain in focus during the zoom-in? If so, why? If not, why not?

3. With your knees pointing in the direction of the start of the pan, pan the camera slowly and smoothly about 180 degrees. Now repeat the same pan with your knees preset as much as possible in the direction of the end point of the pan. Which position makes for a smoother pan? Why?

4. With the automatic white balance turned off, videotape for a few seconds a white object (such as a small white card) outdoors, then repeat the same shot with indoor lighting (such as with your reading lamp shining on it) and then under fluorescent lights. Compare the various color tints of the "white" card. Repeat the same procedure but with the automatic white balance turned on or by white-balancing for each of the illuminations. Now do the colors of the white object look the same in each shot? Why?

5. With a handheld or shoulder-mounted camcorder, follow a friend from behind and videotape him or her while walking along the z-axis. Now do the same while walking backward and having your friend face the camera during the videotaping. Which version made it easier for you to keep the camera steady? Why?

6 Looking Through the Viewfinder

REVIEW OF KEY TERMS

Match each term with its appropriate definition by filling in the corresponding bubble.

1. psychological closure
2. headroom
3. noseroom
4. depth of field

5. field of view
6. z-axis
7. close-up
8. vector

9. medium shot
10. long shot
11. aspect ratio
12. over-the-shoulder shot

A. The relationship of screen width to screen height.

A
○ ○ ○ ○
1 2 3 4
○ ○ ○ ○
5 6 7 8
○ ○ ○ ○
9 10 11 12

B. The portion of a scene visible through a particular lens; its vista.

B
○ ○ ○ ○
1 2 3 4
○ ○ ○ ○
5 6 7 8
○ ○ ○ ○
9 10 11 12

C. Object or any part of it seen at close range.

C
○ ○ ○ ○
1 2 3 4
○ ○ ○ ○
5 6 7 8
○ ○ ○ ○
9 10 11 12

D. Object seen from far away or framed very loosely.

D
○ ○ ○ ○
1 2 3 4
○ ○ ○ ○
5 6 7 8
○ ○ ○ ○
9 10 11 12

PAGE TOTAL [   ]

© 2007 Thomson Wadsworth

1. psychological closure	5. field of view	9. medium shot
2. headroom	6. z-axis	10. long shot
3. noseroom	7. close-up	11. aspect ratio
4. depth of field	8. vector	12. over-the-shoulder shot

E. Mentally filling in missing visual information that will lead to a complete and stable configuration.

E ○ ○ ○ ○
   1 2 3 4
 ○ ○ ○ ○
  5 6 7 8
 ○ ○ ○ ○
  9 10 11 12

F. Object seen from a midrange distance.

F ○ ○ ○ ○
   1 2 3 4
 ○ ○ ○ ○
  5 6 7 8
 ○ ○ ○ ○
  9 10 11 12

G. Indicates screen depth. Extends from camera lens to horizon.

G ○ ○ ○ ○
   1 2 3 4
 ○ ○ ○ ○
  5 6 7 8
 ○ ○ ○ ○
  9 10 11 12

H. The space left between the top of the head and the upper screen edge.

H ○ ○ ○ ○
   1 2 3 4
 ○ ○ ○ ○
  5 6 7 8
 ○ ○ ○ ○
  9 10 11 12

I. The space left in front of a person looking toward the edge of the screen.

I ○ ○ ○ ○
   1 2 3 4
 ○ ○ ○ ○
  5 6 7 8
 ○ ○ ○ ○
  9 10 11 12

J. A directional screen force.

J ○ ○ ○ ○
   1 2 3 4
 ○ ○ ○ ○
  5 6 7 8
 ○ ○ ○ ○
  9 10 11 12

PAGE
TOTAL

1. psychological closure	5. field of view	9. medium shot
2. headroom	6. z-axis	10. long shot
3. noseroom	7. close-up	11. aspect ratio
4. depth of field	8. vector	12. over-the-shoulder shot

K. The area in which all objects, located at different distances from the camera, are in focus.

K
1 2 3 4
5 6 7 8
9 10 11 12

L. Camera looks over the camera-near person's shoulder.

L
1 2 3 4
5 6 7 8
9 10 11 12

PAGE TOTAL

SECTION TOTAL

© 2007 Thomson Wadsworth

REVIEW OF FRAMING A SHOT AND PICTURE COMPOSITION

Select the correct answers and fill in the bubbles with the corresponding numbers.

1. The aspect ratio of the HDTV screen is (13) *4 × 3* (14) *4 × 9* (15) *16 × 9*.

1 ○ ○ ○
   13 14 15

2. Using the following set of numbered images, fill in the corresponding bubble for each of the fields of view or other shot designations listed below.

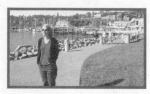
16

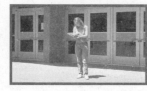
17

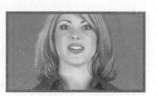
18

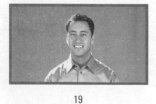
19

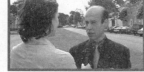
20

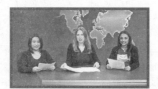
21

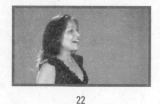
22

23

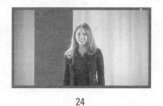
24

a. MS (medium shot)

2a ○ ○ ○ ○ ○
    16 17 18 19 20
○ ○ ○ ○
21 22 23 24

b. LS (long shot)

2b ○ ○ ○ ○ ○
    16 17 18 19 20
○ ○ ○ ○
21 22 23 24

PAGE TOTAL [ ]

c. ELS (extreme long shot)

2c ◯ ◯ ◯ ◯ ◯
    16 17 18 19 20
    ◯ ◯ ◯ ◯
    21 22 23 24

d. bust shot

2d ◯ ◯ ◯ ◯ ◯
    16 17 18 19 20
    ◯ ◯ ◯ ◯
    21 22 23 24

e. ECU (extreme close-up)

2e ◯ ◯ ◯ ◯ ◯
    16 17 18 19 20
    ◯ ◯ ◯ ◯
    21 22 23 24

f. three-shot

2f ◯ ◯ ◯ ◯ ◯
    16 17 18 19 20
    ◯ ◯ ◯ ◯
    21 22 23 24

g. over-the-shoulder shot (O/S)

2g ◯ ◯ ◯ ◯ ◯
    16 17 18 19 20
    ◯ ◯ ◯ ◯
    21 22 23 24

h. CU (close-up)

2h ◯ ◯ ◯ ◯ ◯
    16 17 18 19 20
    ◯ ◯ ◯ ◯
    21 22 23 24

i. knee shot

2i ◯ ◯ ◯ ◯ ◯
    16 17 18 19 20
    ◯ ◯ ◯ ◯
    21 22 23 24

PAGE TOTAL [ ]

3. Evaluate the standard framing of shots in the next eight figures by filling in the bubbles with the corresponding numbers.

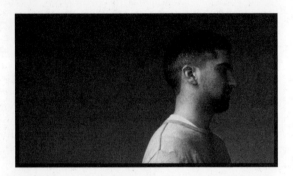

a. This shot is (25) *acceptable* (26) *unacceptable* because it has (27) *too much noseroom* (28) *too little noseroom* (29) *too much headroom* (30) *too much leadroom. (Fill in two bubbles.)*

3a ○ 25 ○ 26
○ 27 ○ 28 ○ 29 ○ 30

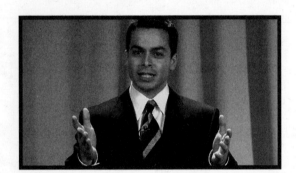

b. This CU is (31) *acceptable* (32) *unacceptable* because it has (33) *no headroom* (34) *too much headroom* (35) *no noseroom* (36) *sufficient clues for closure in off-screen space. (Fill in two bubbles.)*

3b ○ 31 ○ 32
○ 33 ○ 34 ○ 35 ○ 36

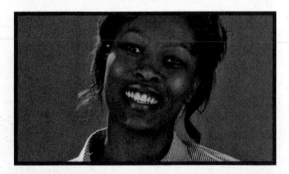

c. This ECU is (37) *acceptable* (38) *unacceptable* because it has (39) *no headroom* (40) *no leadroom* (41) *sufficient clues for closure in off-screen space* (42) *insufficient clues for closure in off-screen space. (Fill in two bubbles.)*

3c ○ 37 ○ 38
○ 39 ○ 40 ○ 41 ○ 42

P A G E
T O T A L [   ]

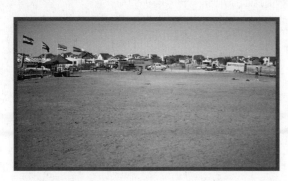

d. This shot makes (43) *good* (44) *poor* use of screen depth. If depth improvement is needed, you should (45) *add foreground objects* (46) *take a tighter shot of the flags.* **(Fill in two bubbles.)**

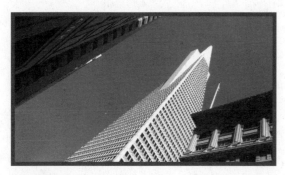

e. This shot is intended to emphasize the dynamic nature of big city buildings. Its framing is (47) *acceptable* (48) *unacceptable.*

3e ◯ 47   ◯ 48

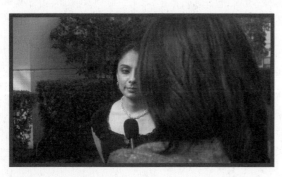

f. This over-the-shoulder shot is (49) *acceptable* (50) *unacceptable.*

3f ◯ 49   ◯ 50

PAGE TOTAL ☐

© 2007 Thomson Wadsworth

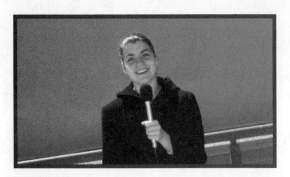

g. The framing of this shot is (51) *acceptable* (52) *unacceptable* because the tilted horizon (53) *makes the shot more dynamic* (54) *is inappropriate in this context.* ***(Fill in two bubbles.)***

3g ◯ ◯
51   52
◯ ◯
53   54

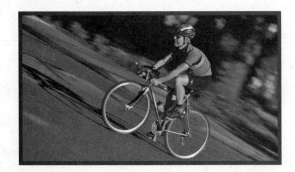

h. The framing of this shot is (55) *acceptable* (56) *unacceptable* because the tilted horizon (57) *makes the shot more dynamic* (58) *is inappropriate in this context.* ***(Fill in two bubbles.)***

3h ◯ ◯
55   56
◯ ◯
57   58

PAGE TOTAL

SECTION TOTAL

REVIEW OF VECTORS AND PSYCHOLOGICAL CLOSURE

1. Identify the specific vectors displayed in the following three figures by filling in the bubbles with the corresponding numbers.

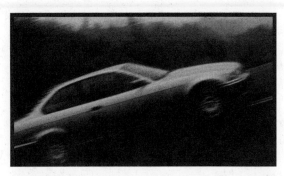

a. This picture shows a prominent (59) *graphic* (60) *index* (61) *motion* vector.

1a ○ 59   ○ 60   ○ 61

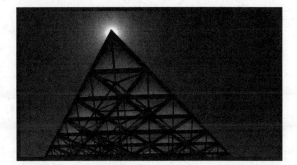

b. This picture shows prominent (62) *graphic* (63) *index* (64) *motion* vectors.

1b ○ 62   ○ 63   ○ 64

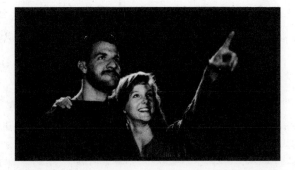

c. This picture shows (65) *graphic* (66) *index* (67) *motion* vectors.

1c ○ 65   ○ 66   ○ 67

PAGE
TOTAL [   ]

© 2007 Thomson Wadsworth

2. Evaluate the following two figures by filling in the bubbles with the corresponding numbers.

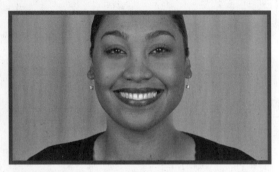

a. The framing of this shot is (68) *acceptable* (69) *unacceptable* because it (70) *leads us to undesirable closure within the frame* (71) *leads us to undesirable closure in off-screen space* (72) *leads us to desirable closure in off-screen space* (73) *prevents closure.* **(Fill in two bubbles.)**

2a ◯ ◯
    68   69

◯ ◯ ◯ ◯
70 71 72 73

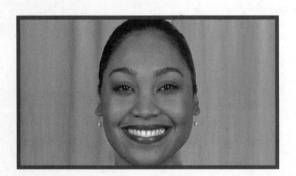

b. The framing of this shot is (74) *acceptable* (75) *unacceptable* because it (76) *leads us to undesirable closure within the frame* (77) *leads us to undesirable closure in off-screen space* (78) *leads us to desirable closure in off-screen space* (79) *prevents closure.* **(Fill in two bubbles.)**

2b ◯ ◯
    74   75

◯ ◯ ◯ ◯
76 77 78 79

PAGE TOTAL ☐

SECTION TOTAL ☐

Course No. _____ Date _____ Name _____

REVIEW OF LENSES, DEPTH OF FIELD, AND Z-AXIS MANIPULATION

Select the correct answers and fill in the bubbles with the corresponding numbers.

1. A wide-angle lens position gives you a relatively (80) *shallow* (81) *wide* (82) *great* depth of field.

2. A narrow-angle lens position gives you a relatively (83) *shallow* (84) *wide* (85) *great* depth of field.

3. The figure below shows the camera zoomed in all the way for a telephoto view and focused on object A. Object B will probably be (86) *in focus* (87) *out of focus.* The depth of field is therefore (88) *great* (89) *shallow.* *(Fill in two bubbles.)*

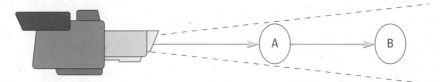

4. The figure below shows the camera zoomed out all the way for a wide-angle view and focused on object A. Object B will probably be (90) *in focus* (91) *out of focus.* The depth of field is therefore (92) *great* (93) *shallow.* *(Fill in two bubbles.)*

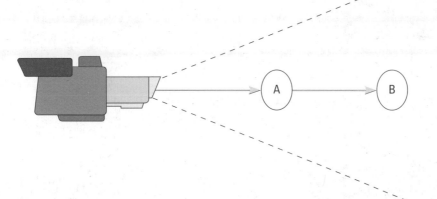

5. The area in which all objects, although located at different distances from the camera, are in focus is called (94) *depth of focus* (95) *field of view* (96) *depth of field.*

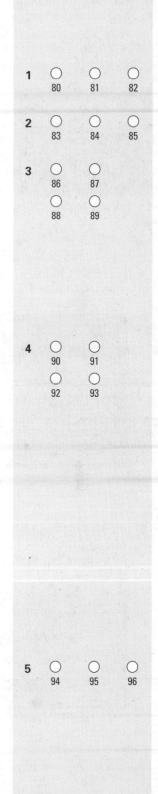

1	○ 80	○ 81	○ 82
2	○ 83	○ 84	○ 85
3	○ 86	○ 87	
	○ 88	○ 89	
4	○ 90	○ 91	
	○ 92	○ 93	
5	○ 94	○ 95	○ 96

PAGE TOTAL [   ]

© 2007 Thomson Wadsworth

Chapter 6 — *Looking Through the Viewfinder*

55

6. The preview monitors for cameras 1, 2, and 3 display the following images. Assuming that all three cameras are positioned right next to one another, what is the approximate zoom position for each? Choose among (97) *wide angle (short focal length)* (98) *normal (medium focal length)* and (99) *narrow angle (long focal length)*.

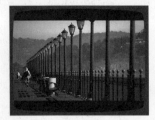
a—Camera 1

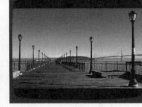
b—Camera 2

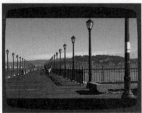
c—Camera 3

6a ○ 97   ○ 98   ○ 99

6b ○ 97   ○ 98   ○ 99

6c ○ 97   ○ 98   ○ 99

7. The screen image below shows that the camera's zoom lens was in a (100) *wide-angle* (101) *narrow-angle* position.

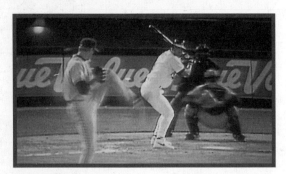

7 ○ 100   ○ 101

8. The screen image below displays a (102) *great* (103) *shallow* depth of field.

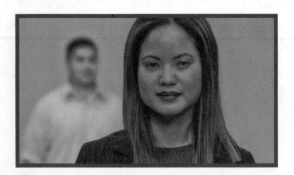

8 ○ 102   ○ 103

PAGE TOTAL ☐

SECTION TOTAL ☐

REVIEW QUIZ

Mark the following statements as true or false by filling in the bubbles in the
T *(for true) or* ***F*** *(for false) column.*

		T	F
1.	The focal length of lenses has considerable influence on the depth of field.	**1** ◯ 104	◯ 105
2.	Wide vistas are easier to frame in the 16 × 9 aspect ratio than the 4 × 3 aspect ratio.	**2** ◯ 106	◯ 107
3.	Wide-angle zoom positions slow down perceived z-axis speed.	**3** ◯ 108	◯ 109
4.	There is no aesthetic difference between a zoom and a dolly.	**4** ◯ 110	◯ 111
5.	When following lateral motion, you should keep as little space as possible between the object and the screen edge toward which the object is moving.	**5** ◯ 112	◯ 113
6.	Psychological closure always ensures good composition.	**6** ◯ 114	◯ 115
7.	In general, video is more of a close-up than a long-shot medium.	**7** ◯ 116	◯ 117
8.	Close-ups normally have a shallow depth of field.	**8** ◯ 118	◯ 119
9.	An effective close-up should provide visual clues for closure in off-screen space.	**9** ◯ 120	◯ 121
10.	You should always try to achieve psychological closure within the TV screen area.	**10** ◯ 122	◯ 123
11.	The aperture of a lens influences the depth of field.	**11** ◯ 124	◯ 125
12.	The focal length of the lens has little influence on how we perceive z-axis blocking.	**12** ◯ 126	◯ 127
13.	Z-axis blocking is especially advantageous for the small screen.	**13** ◯ 128	◯ 129
14.	A tilted horizon line can make the composition less stable and more dynamic.	**14** ◯ 130	◯ 131
15.	Leadroom and noseroom fulfill similar framing (compositional) functions.	**15** ◯ 132	◯ 133

SECTION
TOTAL [   ]

PROBLEM-SOLVING APPLICATIONS

1. With your camcorder in the wide-angle zoom lens position, walk toward an object. Go back to your starting point and this time zoom in on the object. When playing back the two scenes, can you tell which was the dolly and which was the zoom? How?

2. When watching television or a movie, try to figure out what lenses were used for some of the shots. For example, when you see someone running toward the camera yet seemingly not getting closer, what lens was used? Or when you see the happy couple approach the dinner table through the out-of-focus flowers and candles in the foreground, what lens was probably used? Such observations will help you become more aware of focal lengths and their effects. Compare your notes with those of others watching the same program or movie.

3. Your documentary is to show the congestion and the lack of breathing space between the units in a new suburban housing development. When aiming your camera along the street, what zoom lens position would you use? Why?

4. The director wants the foreground object in focus but the background out of focus. How can you accomplish this request?

5. The director tells you, the camera operator, to change from a cross-shot to an over-the-shoulder shot. What does the director mean? How can you accomplish such a shot change?

6. Zoom all the way out with your camcorder, or attach a wide-angle lens (28mm or less focal length) to your 35mm camera, and focus on an object about 4 to 6 feet away from you. Look at the background objects (about 20 feet away from you). Are they visible? Do they appear in fairly sharp focus or are they blurred? Next make the same observations by zooming all the way in or by attaching a telephoto lens (with a focal length of 200mm) to your still camera. Back up and look at the scene. Now relate your observations to depth of field.

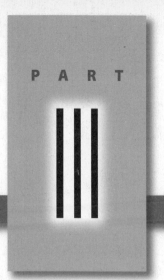

Image Creation: Sound, Light, Graphics, and Effects

PART

III

7 Audio and Sound Control

REVIEW OF KEY TERMS

Match each term with its appropriate definition by filling in the corresponding bubble.

1. omnidirectional
2. pickup pattern
3. hypercardioid
4. polar pattern
5. cardioid
6. unidirectional
7. ribbon microphone

8. dynamic mic
9. windscreen
10. lavaliere
11. VU meter
12. mini plug
13. DAT
14. ATR

15. XLR
16. sweetening
17. jack
18. RCA phono plug
19. condenser microphone
20. fader

A. A professional three-wire connector for audio cables.

A
1	2	3	4	5
6	7	8	9	10
11	12	13	14	15
16	17	18	19	20

B. Acoustic foam rubber that is put over the microphone to cut down wind noise in outdoor use.

B
1	2	3	4	5
6	7	8	9	10
11	12	13	14	15
16	17	18	19	20

PAGE TOTAL

1. omnidirectional	8. dynamic mic	15. XLR
2. pickup pattern	9. windscreen	16. sweetening
3. hypercardioid	10. lavaliere	17. jack
4. polar pattern	11. VU meter	18. RCA phono plug
5. cardioid	12. mini plug	19. condenser microphone
6. unidirectional	13. DAT	20. fader
7. ribbon microphone	14. ATR	

C. A narrow, highly directional pickup pattern.

C
○ ○ ○ ○ ○
1 2 3 4 5
○ ○ ○ ○ ○
6 7 8 9 10
○ ○ ○ ○ ○
11 12 13 14 15
○ ○ ○ ○ ○
16 17 18 19 20

D. A small microphone that is clipped onto clothing.

D
○ ○ ○ ○ ○
1 2 3 4 5
○ ○ ○ ○ ○
6 7 8 9 10
○ ○ ○ ○ ○
11 12 13 14 15
○ ○ ○ ○ ○
16 17 18 19 20

E. Stands for audiotape recorder.

E
○ ○ ○ ○ ○
1 2 3 4 5
○ ○ ○ ○ ○
6 7 8 9 10
○ ○ ○ ○ ○
11 12 13 14 15
○ ○ ○ ○ ○
16 17 18 19 20

F. A heart-shaped pickup pattern.

F
○ ○ ○ ○ ○
1 2 3 4 5
○ ○ ○ ○ ○
6 7 8 9 10
○ ○ ○ ○ ○
11 12 13 14 15
○ ○ ○ ○ ○
16 17 18 19 20

P A G E
T O T A L

Part III — *Image Creation: Sound, Light, Graphics, and Effects*

1. omnidirectional	8. dynamic mic	15. XLR
2. pickup pattern	9. windscreen	16. sweetening
3. hypercardioid	10. lavaliere	17. jack
4. polar pattern	11. VU meter	18. RCA phono plug
5. cardioid	12. mini plug	19. condenser microphone
6. unidirectional	13. DAT	20. fader
7. ribbon microphone	14. ATR	

G. The microphone can best hear sounds that come from the front.

G ① ② ③ ④ ⑤ 1 2 3 4 5
   ⑥ ⑦ ⑧ ⑨ ⑩ 6 7 8 9 10
   ⑪ ⑫ ⑬ ⑭ ⑮ 11 12 13 14 15
   ⑯ ⑰ ⑱ ⑲ ⑳ 16 17 18 19 20

H. The microphone can hear equally well from all directions.

H ① ② ③ ④ ⑤ 1 2 3 4 5
   ⑥ ⑦ ⑧ ⑨ ⑩ 6 7 8 9 10
   ⑪ ⑫ ⑬ ⑭ ⑮ 11 12 13 14 15
   ⑯ ⑰ ⑱ ⑲ ⑳ 16 17 18 19 20

I. The two-dimensional representation of the pickup pattern.

I ① ② ③ ④ ⑤ 1 2 3 4 5
   ⑥ ⑦ ⑧ ⑨ ⑩ 6 7 8 9 10
   ⑪ ⑫ ⑬ ⑭ ⑮ 11 12 13 14 15
   ⑯ ⑰ ⑱ ⑲ ⑳ 16 17 18 19 20

J. A relatively rugged microphone. Good for outdoor use.

J ① ② ③ ④ ⑤ 1 2 3 4 5
   ⑥ ⑦ ⑧ ⑨ ⑩ 6 7 8 9 10
   ⑪ ⑫ ⑬ ⑭ ⑮ 11 12 13 14 15
   ⑯ ⑰ ⑱ ⑲ ⑳ 16 17 18 19 20

PAGE TOTAL [ ]

1. omnidirectional	8. dynamic mic	15. XLR
2. pickup pattern	9. windscreen	16. sweetening
3. hypercardioid	10. lavaliere	17. jack
4. polar pattern	11. VU meter	18. RCA phono plug
5. cardioid	12. mini plug	19. condenser microphone
6. unidirectional	13. DAT	20. fader
7. ribbon microphone	14. ATR	

K. High-quality, highly sensitive microphone for critical sound pickup. Produces warm sound.

K

L. The territory around the microphone within which the mic can hear well.

L

M. Small connector normally used for most consumer video and audio equipment.

M

N. Tiny connector used for some consumer audio equipment.

N

PAGE TOTAL

Part III — *Image Creation: Sound, Light, Graphics, and Effects*

1. omnidirectional	8. dynamic mic	15. XLR
2. pickup pattern	9. windscreen	16. sweetening
3. hypercardioid	10. lavaliere	17. jack
4. polar pattern	11. VU meter	18. RCA phono plug
5. cardioid	12. mini plug	19. condenser microphone
6. unidirectional	13. DAT	20. fader
7. ribbon microphone	14. ATR	

O. A socket or receptacle for a connector.

P. A sliding volume control.

Q. Stands for digital audiotape.

R. Manipulating recorded sound in postproduction.

O 1 2 3 4 5 6 7 8 9 10 11 12 13 14 15 16 17 18 19 20

P 1 2 3 4 5 6 7 8 9 10 11 12 13 14 15 16 17 18 19 20

Q 1 2 3 4 5 6 7 8 9 10 11 12 13 14 15 16 17 18 19 20

R 1 2 3 4 5 6 7 8 9 10 11 12 13 14 15 16 17 18 19 20

PAGE TOTAL

© 2007 Thomson Wadsworth

1. omnidirectional	8. dynamic mic	15. XLR
2. pickup pattern	9. windscreen	16. sweetening
3. hypercardioid	10. lavaliere	17. jack
4. polar pattern	11. VU meter	18. RCA phono plug
5. cardioid	12. mini plug	19. condenser microphone
6. unidirectional	13. DAT	20. fader
7. ribbon microphone	14. ATR	

S. Measures volume units, the relative loudness of amplified sound.

S
1 2 3 4 5
6 7 8 9 10
11 12 13 14 15
16 17 18 19 20

T. High-quality microphone with a battery power supply.

T
1 2 3 4 5
6 7 8 9 10
11 12 13 14 15
16 17 18 19 20

PAGE TOTAL

SECTION TOTAL

REVIEW OF SOUND-GENERATING ELEMENTS AND SOUND PICKUP

Select the correct answers and fill in the bubbles with the corresponding numbers.

1. Fill in the bubbles whose numbers correspond with the polar patterns in the following figure.

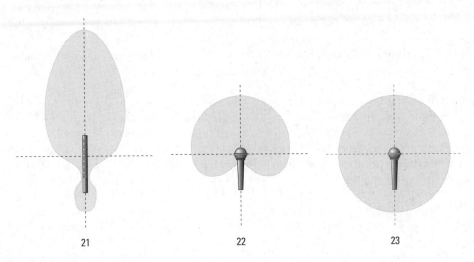

21   22   23

    a. omnidirectional

    b. cardioid

    c. hypercardioid

2. Select the three types of microphones as classified by how they are made—their sound-generating element: (24) *cardioid* (25) *ribbon* (26) *omnidirectional* (27) *dynamic* (28) *condenser* (29) *unidirectional*. **(Fill in three bubbles.)**

3. A shotgun mic has a pickup pattern that is (30) *omnidirectional* (31) *unidirectional (hypercardioid)* (32) *nondirectional*.

4. The microphone that needs a special power supply (usually a battery) to amplify the sound signal in the microphone is (33) *dynamic* (34) *ribbon* (35) *condenser*.

5. To eliminate sudden plosive sounds when speaking close to the microphone, use a (36) *pop filter* (37) *windscreen* (38) *ribbon filter*.

6. The most rugged microphones that work well outdoors are (39) *dynamic* (40) *ribbon* (41) *condenser*.

1a	○ 21	○ 22	○ 23
1b	○ 21	○ 22	○ 23
1c	○ 21	○ 22	○ 23
2	○ 24	○ 25	○ 26
	○ 27	○ 28	○ 29
3	○ 30	○ 31	○ 32
4	○ 33	○ 34	○ 35
5	○ 36	○ 37	○ 38
6	○ 39	○ 40	○ 41

SECTION TOTAL [   ]

REVIEW OF MICROPHONE USE

Select the correct answers and fill in the bubbles with the corresponding numbers.

1. Boom microphones (fishpole and perambulator) normally have (42) *a cardioid* (43) *an omnidirectional* (44) *a hyper- or supercardioid* pickup pattern.

   | 1 | ○ 42 | ○ 43 | ○ 44 |

2. The hand microphones used in ENG normally have (45) *an omnidirectional* (46) *a bidirectional* (47) *a hyper- or supercardioid* pickup pattern.

   | 2 | ○ 45 | ○ 46 | ○ 47 |

3. News anchors usually use (48) *lavaliere* (49) *hand* (50) *boom* mics.

   | 3 | ○ 48 | ○ 49 | ○ 50 |

4. The high-quality hand microphone normally used by singers is a (51) *dynamic* (52) *supercardioid* (53) *condenser* microphone.

   | 4 | ○ 51 | ○ 52 | ○ 53 |

5. You are to set up microphones for a six-member panel discussion. All participants sit in a row at a long table. Normally, you would use (54) *boom* (55) *hand* (56) *desk* mics for this production.

   | 5 | ○ 54 | ○ 55 | ○ 56 |

6. When using a shotgun mic outdoors, you should cover it with a (57) *windscreen* (58) *styrofoam case* (59) *windsock*. **(Multiple answers are possible.)**

   | 6 | ○ 57 | ○ 58 | ○ 59 |

7. When interviewing a runner after a race, the most flexible microphone is the (60) *boom* (61) *hand* (62) *lavaliere* mic.

   | 7 | ○ 60 | ○ 61 | ○ 62 |

8. The most useful mic for a singer in a band is the (63) *boom* (64) *stand* (65) *lavaliere* mic.

   | 8 | ○ 63 | ○ 64 | ○ 65 |

9. In noisy surroundings, the field reporter must speak (66) *across* (67) *into* (68) *at a right angle to* the hand mic.

   | 9 | ○ 66 | ○ 67 | ○ 68 |

10. When using a shotgun mic on a fishpole, you can pick up the sound (69) *only from above* (70) *only from below* (71) *from above or below* the source.

    | 10 | ○ 69 | ○ 70 | ○ 71 |

SECTION TOTAL

REVIEW OF SOUND CONTROL

Select the correct answers and fill in the bubbles with the corresponding numbers.

1. The variety of quality controls on an audio console is (72) *greater than* (73) *the same as* (74) *less than* the quality controls on an audio mixer.

2. Overloading the volume of the incoming sound signal will result in (75) *distorted sound* (76) *earache* (77) *damage to the VU meter.*

3. The test tone at the beginning of a videotape recording should be (78) *–1 VU* (79) *+1 VU* (80) *0 VU.*

4. For digital recording, the test tone should be (81) *0 VU* (82) *below 0 VU* (83) *above 0 VU.*

Fill in the bubble whose number corresponds with the number identifying the equipment shown in the following two figures.

5. The place that marks the beginning of the "overload" zone is (84) *–5 VU* (85) *–2 VU* (86) *0 VU.*

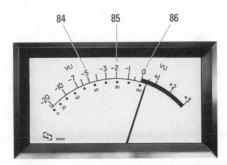

6. The various heads in the head assembly shown in the following figure are:

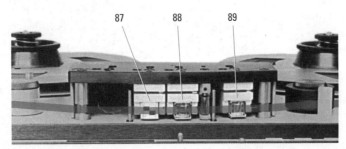

a. playback head

b. erase head

c. record head

1	○ 72	○ 73	○ 74
2	○ 75	○ 76	○ 77
3	○ 78	○ 79	○ 80
4	○ 81	○ 82	○ 83
5	○ 84	○ 85	○ 86
6a	○ 87	○ 88	○ 89
6b	○ 87	○ 88	○ 89
6c	○ 87	○ 88	○ 89

PAGE TOTAL [　　　]

7. When plugging a mic into a camcorder or mixer, the mic cable must be plugged into the (90) *line-level* (91) *remote* (92) *mic-level* jack.

8. The various audio connectors as shown in this figure are:

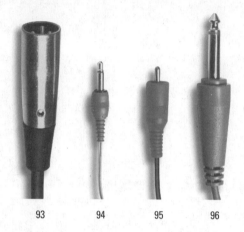

93   94   95   96

a. RCA phono plug

b. mini plug

c. phone plug

d. XLR

9. Most professional mic cables use (97) *RCA phono* (98) *mini plug* (99) *XLR connectors.*

10. When recording digital audio, the VU meter (100) *can* (101) *can occasionally* (102) *should never* spill into the overload zone.

REVIEW OF SOUND RECORDING AND AESTHETICS

Select the correct answers and fill in the bubbles with the corresponding numbers.

1. An analog 24-track recorder needs the following number of head assemblies (erase, record, and playback): (103) *12* (104) *24* (105) *48.*

   1 ◯ ◯ ◯
       103   104   105

2. A CD contains audio information in (106) *laser* (107) *analog* (108) *digital* form.

   2 ◯ ◯ ◯
       106   107   108

3. Matching audio and video energies means to (109) *adjust the strength of audio signals to that of video signals* (110) *use special digital video and audio devices* (111) *have high- or low-energy audio accompany high- or low-energy video.*

   3 ◯ ◯ ◯
       109   110   111

4. The figure/ground principle in audio refers to (112) *a person speaking while moving against a stable background* (113) *making the principal sound source as loud as the background sounds* (114) *separating the principal sound source from the background sounds through a higher volume.*

   4 ◯ ◯ ◯
       112   113   114

SECTION TOTAL ☐

Mark the following statements as true or false by filling in the bubbles in the
T (for true) or **F** (for false) column.

		T	F
1.	Because lavaliere microphones are highly sensitive, they work best when hidden under a shirt or blouse.	**1** ○ 115	○ 116
2.	Dynamic mics are generally less sensitive to shock and temperature extremes than are condenser mics.	**2** ○ 117	○ 118
3.	Lavaliere microphones are useful for news anchors.	**3** ○ 119	○ 120
4.	To test whether a microphone is turned on, you should blow into it.	**4** ○ 121	○ 122
5.	DAT cassettes cannot be played on regular (analog) cassette players.	**5** ○ 123	○ 124
6.	Riding gain means adjusting the VU meter so that it continuously reads *0* regardless of the input audio levels.	**6** ○ 125	○ 126
7.	In EFP you should try to mix the sounds as carefully as possible with the use of a portable mixer.	**7** ○ 127	○ 128
8.	Regardless of whether you work with a mixer or an audio console, each input has its own pot (fader).	**8** ○ 129	○ 130
9.	Digital audio can be recorded on a DAT recorder but not on videotape.	**9** ○ 131	○ 132
10.	Digital sound is less sensitive to distortion than analog sound when riding gain between 0 and +1 VU.	**10** ○ 133	○ 134
11.	Because there are adapters, you don't have to worry about the cable connectors' fitting the equipment jacks.	**11** ○ 135	○ 136
12.	A fishpole mic is the best pickup method for a panel discussion.	**12** ○ 137	○ 138
13.	You should always use AGC when doing a field pickup.	**13** ○ 139	○ 140
14.	When riding gain, you should keep the VU needle between 60 and 100 (–5 and 0).	**14** ○ 141	○ 142
15.	Line-level inputs are used for relatively high-level inputs.	**15** ○ 143	○ 144
16.	All microphones are insensitive to shock once they are turned off.	**16** ○ 145	○ 146
17.	In sound calibration, you need to adjust the VU meter on the video recorder so that it matches the 0 VU tone fed by the audio console.	**17** ○ 147	○ 148
18.	Once you use an external microphone, you should turn off the camera mic.	**18** ○ 149	○ 150

SECTION TOTAL [ ]

PROBLEM-SOLVING APPLICATIONS

1. The new PA tells you that the audio engineer of his former employer used lavaliere microphones exclusively on the actors of a college play because lavs would provide excellent sound perspective without driving the audio console operator crazy. Do you agree with this audio engineer? If so, why? If not, why not?

2. While riding gain during a live-on-tape pickup of a small rock band, the director is concerned about overmodulation when the VU meters occasionally peak into the +1 red zone. What is your response?

3. You are doing a documentary on police patrols in your city. You first want to hear the conversations and the police radio inside the patrol car and then capture the sounds of possible conversations, yelling, or any other audio when the officers leave the patrol car to confront a suspect. What microphones would you need for optimal sound pickup in these situations?

4. During a short segment of an EFP in an auto assembly plant, the new PA wonders why the audio people do not try mixing the ambient sounds with the voices of the reporter and the plant supervisor right on the spot. He feels that mixing in the field would eliminate a great deal of postproduction sweetening. What are your comments?

5. You are in charge of audio for a show that consists of several intimate numbers by a singer and a small band. After the rehearsal an observer in the control room tells you that the singer holds the mic during the softer passages much too close to her mouth and that she should hold the mic much lower and sing "across" rather than into it. What is your reaction? Why?

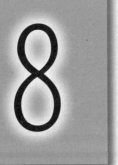

Light, Color, and Lighting

REVIEW OF KEY TERMS

Match each term with its appropriate definition by filling in the corresponding bubble.

1. directional light
2. diffused light
3. baselight
4. lux
5. foot-candle
6. attached shadow
7. cast shadow

8. falloff
9. additive primary colors
10. color temperature
11. Kelvin
12. spotlight
13. floodlight
14. contrast

15. photographic principle
16. key light
17. fill light
18. back light
19. background light
20. light plot

A. Illumination of the set pieces and the backdrop.

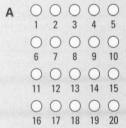

B. The standard scale for measuring color temperature.

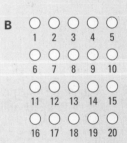

PAGE
TOTAL

1. directional light	8. falloff	15. photographic principle
2. diffused light	9. additive primary colors	16. key light
3. baselight	10. color temperature	17. fill light
4. lux	11. Kelvin	18. back light
5. foot-candle	12. spotlight	19. background light
6. attached shadow	13. floodlight	20. light plot
7. cast shadow	14. contrast	

C. Shadow that is produced by an object and thrown on another surface. It can be independent of the object.

C
○ ○ ○ ○ ○
1   2   3   4   5
○ ○ ○ ○ ○
6   7   8   9   10
○ ○ ○ ○ ○
11   12   13   14   15
○ ○ ○ ○ ○
16   17   18   19   20

D. Lighting instrument that produces directional, relatively undiffused light.

D
○ ○ ○ ○ ○
1   2   3   4   5
○ ○ ○ ○ ○
6   7   8   9   10
○ ○ ○ ○ ○
11   12   13   14   15
○ ○ ○ ○ ○
16   17   18   19   20

E. Lighting instrument that produces diffused light.

E
○ ○ ○ ○ ○
1   2   3   4   5
○ ○ ○ ○ ○
6   7   8   9   10
○ ○ ○ ○ ○
11   12   13   14   15
○ ○ ○ ○ ○
16   17   18   19   20

F. Even, nondirectional light necessary for the camera to operate optimally. Refers to the overall light intensity.

F
○ ○ ○ ○ ○
1   2   3   4   5
○ ○ ○ ○ ○
6   7   8   9   10
○ ○ ○ ○ ○
11   12   13   14   15
○ ○ ○ ○ ○
16   17   18   19   20

PAGE TOTAL ☐

76

1. directional light
2. diffused light
3. baselight
4. lux
5. foot-candle
6. attached shadow
7. cast shadow
8. falloff
9. additive primary colors
10. color temperature
11. Kelvin
12. spotlight
13. floodlight
14. contrast
15. photographic principle
16. key light
17. fill light
18. back light
19. background light
20. light plot

G. The standard arrangement of key, back, and fill lights, with the back light opposite the camera and directly behind the object, and the key and fill lights on opposite sides of the camera and to the front and side of the object.

G
1 2 3 4 5
6 7 8 9 10
11 12 13 14 15
16 17 18 19 20

H. The speed (degree) with which a light picture portion turns into shadow areas. It can be fast or slow.

H
1 2 3 4 5
6 7 8 9 10
11 12 13 14 15
16 17 18 19 20

I. The difference between the lightest and darkest spot in a picture.

I
1 2 3 4 5
6 7 8 9 10
11 12 13 14 15
16 17 18 19 20

J. Light that illuminates a relatively large area with an indistinct light beam.

J
1 2 3 4 5
6 7 8 9 10
11 12 13 14 15
16 17 18 19 20

PAGE
TOTAL

1. directional light	8. falloff	15. photographic principle
2. diffused light	9. additive primary colors	16. key light
3. baselight	10. color temperature	17. fill light
4. lux	11. Kelvin	18. back light
5. foot-candle	12. spotlight	19. background light
6. attached shadow	13. floodlight	20. light plot
7. cast shadow	14. contrast	

K. A plan, similar to a floor plan, that shows the type and the location of the lighting instruments relative to the scene to be illuminated and the general direction of the beams.

K
1 2 3 4 5
6 7 8 9 10
11 12 13 14 15
16 17 18 19 20

L. Illumination from behind the subject and opposite the camera.

L
1 2 3 4 5
6 7 8 9 10
11 12 13 14 15
16 17 18 19 20

M. Shadow that is on the object itself. It cannot be seen independent of the object.

M
1 2 3 4 5
6 7 8 9 10
11 12 13 14 15
16 17 18 19 20

N. Light that illuminates a relatively small area with a distinct light beam.

N
1 2 3 4 5
6 7 8 9 10
11 12 13 14 15
16 17 18 19 20

PAGE TOTAL

1. **directional light**	8. **falloff**	15. **photographic principle**
2. **diffused light**	9. **additive primary colors**	16. **key light**
3. **baselight**	10. **color temperature**	17. **fill light**
4. **lux**	11. **Kelvin**	18. **back light**
5. **foot-candle**	12. **spotlight**	19. **background light**
6. **attached shadow**	13. **floodlight**	20. **light plot**
7. **cast shadow**	14. **contrast**	

O. Red, green, and blue.

P. Additional light on the opposite side of the camera from the key light to illuminate shadow areas and thereby reduce falloff.

Q. Principal source of illumination.

R. The standard European unit for measuring light intensity.

PAGE TOTAL

Chapter 8 — Light, Color, and Lighting

1. directional light	8. falloff	15. photographic principle
2. diffused light	9. additive primary colors	16. key light
3. baselight	10. color temperature	17. fill light
4. lux	11. Kelvin	18. back light
5. foot-candle	12. spotlight	19. background light
6. attached shadow	13. floodlight	20. light plot
7. cast shadow	14. contrast	

S. The American unit for measuring light intensity.

S
○ ○ ○ ○ ○
1 2 3 4 5
○ ○ ○ ○ ○
6 7 8 9 10
○ ○ ○ ○ ○
11 12 13 14 15
○ ○ ○ ○ ○
16 17 18 19 20

T. Relative reddishness or bluishness of light, as measured on the Kelvin scale.

T
○ ○ ○ ○ ○
1 2 3 4 5
○ ○ ○ ○ ○
6 7 8 9 10
○ ○ ○ ○ ○
11 12 13 14 15
○ ○ ○ ○ ○
16 17 18 19 20

P A G E TOTAL

SECTION TOTAL

REVIEW OF LIGHT, SHADOWS, AND COLOR

Select the correct answers and fill in the bubbles with the corresponding numbers.

1. Electronic white balance (21) *makes a white object look white on the monitor regardless of the relative color temperature of the light* (22) *controls extremely bright spots in the picture* (23) *adjusts the brightness in the viewfinder.*

   1 ○ 21   ○ 22   ○ 23

2. Baselight levels are measured in (24) *lux* (25) *foot-candles* (26) *f-stops.* **(Multiple answers are possible.)**

   2 ○ 24   ○ 25   ○ 26

3. One foot-candle is approximately (27) *5* (28) *10* (29) *15* lux.

   3 ○ 27   ○ 28   ○ 29

4. A high color temperature means that the light has a (30) *reddish* (31) *bluish* (32) *greenish* tinge.

   4 ○ 30   ○ 31   ○ 32

5. Fast falloff means that there is (33) *a great difference between the light side and the attached shadow side of the object* (34) *a great difference between the light side and the cast shadow side of the object* (35) *little difference between the light side and the attached shadow side of the object.*

   5 ○ 33   ○ 34   ○ 35

6. When all three electron guns in a color monitor hit the three additive color dots at maximum intensity, the screen will be (36) *white* (37) *black* (38) *multicolored.*

   6 ○ 36   ○ 37   ○ 38

7. The standard color temperature for outdoor lighting is (39) *3,200K* (40) *3,600K* (41) *5,600K.*

   7 ○ 39   ○ 40   ○ 41

8. When lowering the color temperature, the white light becomes more (42) *reddish* (43) *greenish* (44) *bluish.*

   8 ○ 42   ○ 43   ○ 44

9. The standard color temperature for indoor lighting is (45) *3,200K* (46) *3,600K* (47) *5,600K.*

   9 ○ 45   ○ 46   ○ 47

10. When lighting for slow falloff in large areas, you should use predominantly (48) *directional* (49) *diffused* (50) *high-color-temperature* light.

    10 ○ 48   ○ 49   ○ 50

11. When measuring incident light, you must stand next to the lighted object and point the light meter (51) *toward the camera lens* (52) *toward the object* (53) *toward the background.*

    11 ○ 51   ○ 52   ○ 53

12. When measuring reflected light, you must stand next to the lighted object and point the light meter (54) *toward the camera lens* (55) *toward the object* (56) *into the lights.*

    12 ○ 54   ○ 55   ○ 56

13. Contrast is measured by reading the (57) *brightest and darkest areas in the scene* (58) *highest and lowest color temperatures in a scene* (59) *foreground light and background light.*

    13 ○ 57   ○ 58   ○ 59

SECTION TOTAL ☐

REVIEW OF LIGHTING INSTRUMENTS

1. Fill in the bubbles whose numbers correspond with the appropriate lighting instruments shown below:

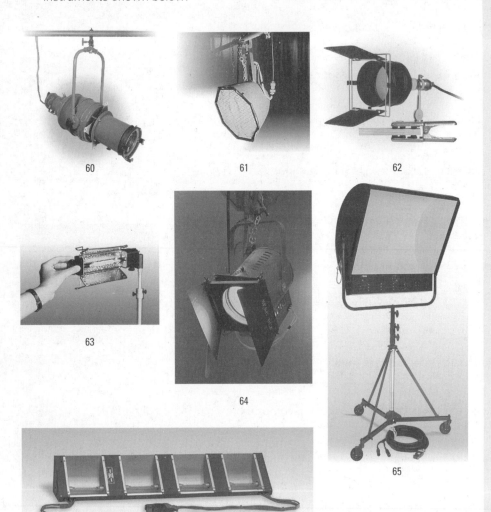

60

61

62

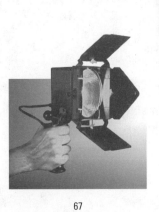

63

64

65

66

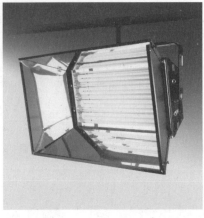

67

68

Course No. _____ Date _____ Name _____

a. softlight

1a	60	61	62	63	64
	65	66	67	68	

b. Fresnel spotlight

1b	60	61	62	63	64
	65	66	67	68	

c. fluorescent bank

1c	60	61	62	63	64
	65	66	67	68	

d. Omni light

1d	60	61	62	63	64
	65	66	67	68	

e. strip, or cyc, light

1e	60	61	62	63	64
	65	66	67	68	

f. scoop

1f	60	61	62	63	64
	65	66	67	68	

g. ellipsoidal spotlight

1g	60	61	62	63	64
	65	66	67	68	

h. EFP floodlight (Tota light)

1h	60	61	62	63	64
	65	66	67	68	

i. clip light

1i	60	61	62	63	64
	65	66	67	68	

PAGE
TOTAL

Select the correct answers and fill in the bubbles with the corresponding numbers.

2. To flood (spread) the light beam of a Fresnel spotlight, you need to move the lamp-reflector unit (69) *toward* (70) *away from* the lens; to focus the beam more narrowly, move it (71) *toward* (72) *away from* the lens. *(Fill in two bubbles.)*

2	○ 69	○ 70
	○ 71	○ 72

3. The flooded beam has (73) *more* (74) *less* intensity than the focused beam.

3	○ 73	○ 74

4. Open-face portable spotlights have (75) *a Fresnel zoom lens* (76) *no lens* and (77) *a small focus control* (78) *no focus control.* *(Fill in two bubbles.)*

4	○ 75	○ 76
	○ 77	○ 78

5. A scoop has (79) *a Fresnel lens* (80) *no lens* and (81) *a focus control* (82) *no focus control.* *(Fill in two bubbles.)*

5	○ 79	○ 80
	○ 81	○ 82

PAGE TOTAL [ ]

SECTION TOTAL [ ]

REVIEW OF LIGHTING TECHNIQUES

Select the correct answers and fill in the bubbles with the corresponding numbers.

1. The arrangement of lighting instruments shown in the figure below is generally called (83) *triangle lighting or the basic photographic principle* (84) *three-point lighting* (85) *photographic lighting* (86) *the field lighting principle.*

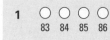

1 ◯ ◯ ◯ ◯
83 84 85 86

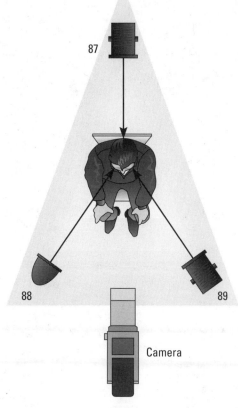

Camera

2. Fill in the bubbles whose numbers correspond with the functions of lighting instruments shown in the figure above and whether they are usually (90) *spotlights* or (91) *floodlights*. **(Fill in two bubbles.)**

a. key

b. back

c. fill

2a ◯   ◯   ◯
    87   88   89
       ◯   ◯
       90   91

2b ◯   ◯   ◯
    87   88   89
       ◯   ◯
       90   91

2c ◯   ◯   ◯
    87   88   89
       ◯   ◯
       90   91

PAGE
TOTAL [ ]

© 2007 Thomson Wadsworth

3. What major light sources were used for illuminating the on-screen person in the following three pictures? In the diagrams, circle the instrument or instruments used, then fill in the bubbles whose numbers correspond with the instruments used to light the subject. *(Multiple answers are possible.)*

a.

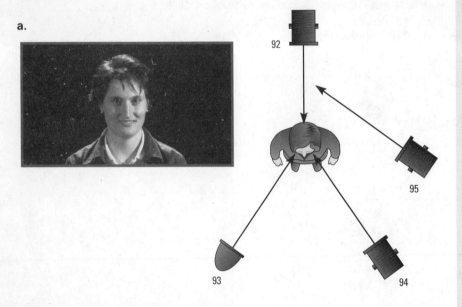

b.

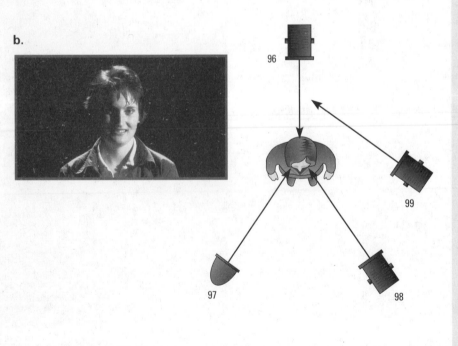

P A G E
T O T A L

Part III — *Image Creation: Sound, Light, Graphics, and Effects*

c.

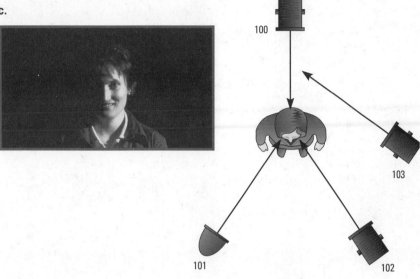

100

103

101   102

d.

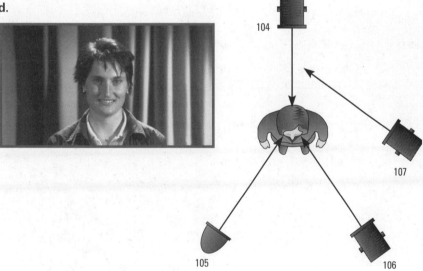

104

107

105   106

3c ◯ ◯ ◯ ◯
100 101 102 103

3d ◯ ◯ ◯ ◯
104 105 106 107

4. When shooting an ENG interview in bright sunlight, the most convenient fill light is a (108) *large spot* (109) *scoop* (110) *reflector*.

5. Having somebody stand in front of a brightly illuminated building will (111) *provide much needed back light* (112) *help separate the person from the background* (113) *cause an undesirable silhouette effect*.

6. When trying to match the color temperature of outdoor light coming into a room through a window with that of your standard portable floodlights, you need to (114) *lower* (115) *raise* the color temperature of your indoor lights by putting (116) *an amber (warm orange)* (117) *a light blue* gel (filter) in front of all indoor instruments. *(Fill in two bubbles.)*

4 ◯   ◯   ◯
108   109   110

5 ◯   ◯   ◯
111   112   113

6 ◯   ◯
114   115
◯   ◯
116   117

PAGE
TOTAL ☐

SECTION
TOTAL ☐

REVIEW QUIZ

Mark the following statements as true or false by filling in the bubbles in the
T *(for true) or* ***F*** *(for false) column.*

		T	F
1.	An amber or orange gel in front of a lighting instrument will raise its color temperature.	1 ○ 118	○ 119
2.	Floodlights are the quickest way to illuminate a large area with even light.	2 ○ 120	○ 121
3.	The basic photographic principle uses a key light, a fill light, and a spotlight.	3 ○ 122	○ 123
4.	The more fill light, the slower the falloff.	4 ○ 124	○ 125
5.	All professional floodlights have Fresnel lenses.	5 ○ 126	○ 127
6.	Color temperature refers to how hotly a light burns.	6 ○ 128	○ 129
7.	You can use a floodlight for a key.	7 ○ 130	○ 131
8.	Back lights and background lights fulfill similar functions.	8 ○ 132	○ 133
9.	The background light must strike the background from the same side as the key light.	9 ○ 134	○ 135
10.	The best lighting instrument for EFP is the 2,000-watt Fresnel spotlight.	10 ○ 136	○ 137
11.	C-clamps are built for mounting spotlights but not floodlights.	11 ○ 138	○ 139
12.	Barn doors are primarily used to slow down falloff.	12 ○ 140	○ 141
13.	Normally, small ENG/EFP lights, such as the Lowel Omni light, have no lens.	13 ○ 142	○ 143
14.	We measure color temperature on the Kelvin scale.	14 ○ 144	○ 145
15.	Softlights can focus their light beam.	15 ○ 146	○ 147
16.	Fluorescent banks produce fast falloff.	16 ○ 148	○ 149
17.	We measure incident light by pointing the light meter close to the lighted object.	17 ○ 150	○ 151
18.	Backlights can easily be substituted by a reflector.	18 ○ 152	○ 153
19.	An overcast day produces low-contrast lighting.	19 ○ 154	○ 155
20.	High-key lighting means that the key light is situated above eye level.	20 ○ 156	○ 157

PAGE
TOTAL

PROBLEM-SOLVING APPLICATIONS

1. You are asked to do the lighting for a shampoo commercial. The director wants you to make the model's blond hair look especially brilliant and glamorous. Which of the three instruments of the lighting triangle needs special attention to achieve the desired result?

2. You have very little time to light a five-member panel discussion in the multipurpose room of the local elementary school. The board members sit side-by-side behind a long table. What lighting type would you employ? What instruments would you use? Why?

3. The director of a studio interview with a prize-winning actor suggests using a softlight as the key instead of a Fresnel spot. What is your reaction? Be specific.

4. You are asked to videotape the president of a new computer company who wants to talk to her employees from behind her desk. The vice president tells you not to worry about the large window behind the president's chair because you can use the daylight streaming through the window as interesting back light. What is your reaction? What problems, if any, do you anticipate? What solutions would you suggest?

5. The novice assistant director is very worried about videotaping the high-school graduation ceremony. He said that the overcast sky will cause fast falloff and is prone to color distortion in the shadow areas. What is your reaction? Why?

9 Graphics and Effects

REVIEW OF KEY TERMS

Match each term with its appropriate definition by filling in the corresponding bubble.

1. **ESS system**
2. **DVE**
3. **super**
4. **C.G.**

5. **key**
6. **wipe**
7. **chroma key**
8. **aspect ratio**

9. **essential area**
10. **matte key**

A. A transition in which one image gradually replaces the other on the screen in various configurations.

A ○ ○ ○ ○ ○
   1 2 3 4 5
   ○ ○ ○ ○ ○
   6 7 8 9 10

B. The section of the screen seen by the home viewer despite a badly aligned TV set.

B ○ ○ ○ ○ ○
   1 2 3 4 5
   ○ ○ ○ ○ ○
   6 7 8 9 10

C. Stores many still video frames in digital form for easy access.

C ○ ○ ○ ○ ○
   1 2 3 4 5
   ○ ○ ○ ○ ○
   6 7 8 9 10

D. The width-to-height relationship of a video screen.

D ○ ○ ○ ○ ○
   1 2 3 4 5
   ○ ○ ○ ○ ○
   6 7 8 9 10

E. A computer dedicated to the creation of letters and numbers.

E ○ ○ ○ ○ ○
   1 2 3 4 5
   ○ ○ ○ ○ ○
   6 7 8 9 10

PAGE TOTAL [ ]

1. ESS system	5. key	9. essential area
2. DVE	6. wipe	10. matte key
3. super	7. chroma key	
4. C.G.	8. aspect ratio	

F. Letters of a keyed title are filled with gray or a specific color through a third video source.

F ○ ○ ○ ○ ○
   1 2 3 4 5
   ○ ○ ○ ○ ○
   6 7 8 9 10

G. Special effect that uses color (usually blue) for the backdrop of the source (foreground picture). All blue areas are replaced by the base picture.

G ○ ○ ○ ○ ○
   1 2 3 4 5
   ○ ○ ○ ○ ○
   6 7 8 9 10

H. Analog electronic visual effect in which letters are cut into a base picture, making the letters seem to be printed on top of the background scene.

H ○ ○ ○ ○ ○
   1 2 3 4 5
   ○ ○ ○ ○ ○
   6 7 8 9 10

I. Video effects generated by a computer.

I ○ ○ ○ ○ ○
   1 2 3 4 5
   ○ ○ ○ ○ ○
   6 7 8 9 10

J. The simultaneous overlay of two pictures on the same screen.

J ○ ○ ○ ○ ○
   1 2 3 4 5
   ○ ○ ○ ○ ○
   6 7 8 9 10

PAGE TOTAL ☐

SECTION TOTAL ☐

REVIEW OF STANDARD ELECTRONIC EFFECTS

1. Fill in the bubbles whose numbers correspond with the appropriate key effects shown in the following figures.

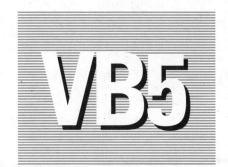

11

12

13

14

a. matte key

1a ◯ ◯ ◯ ◯
    11 12 13 14

b. outline mode

1b ◯ ◯ ◯ ◯
    11 12 13 14

c. drop-shadow mode

1c ◯ ◯ ◯ ◯
    11 12 13 14

d. edge mode

1d ◯ ◯ ◯ ◯
    11 12 13 14

PAGE TOTAL

2. Fill in the bubbles whose numbers correspond with the buttons you would have to press on the pattern selector to create the various effects (a through e) illustrated in the following figures. *(Note that some numbered buttons do not apply.)*

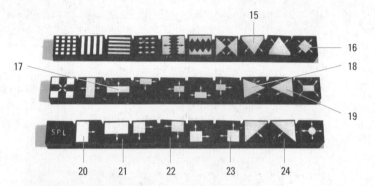

a.

2a ◯ ◯ ◯ ◯ ◯
    15 16 17 18 19
    ◯ ◯ ◯ ◯ ◯
    20 21 22 23 24

b.

2b ◯ ◯ ◯ ◯ ◯
    15 16 17 18 19
    ◯ ◯ ◯ ◯ ◯
    20 21 22 23 24

c.

2c ◯ ◯ ◯ ◯ ◯
    15 16 17 18 19
    ◯ ◯ ◯ ◯ ◯
    20 21 22 23 24

PAGE
TOTAL [   ]

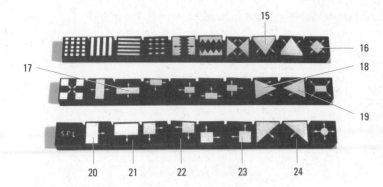

15
16
17
18
19
20 21 22 23 24

d.

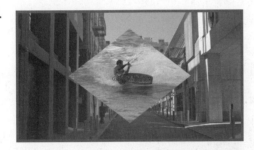

e.

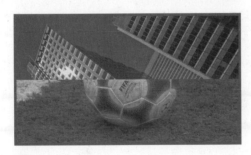

2d ○ ○ ○ ○ ○
    15 16 17 18 19
    ○ ○ ○ ○ ○
    20 21 22 23 24

2e ○ ○ ○ ○ ○
    15 16 17 18 19
    ○ ○ ○ ○ ○
    20 21 22 23 24

PAGE
TOTAL

3. Fill in the bubbles whose numbers correspond with the appropriate electronic effects shown in the following figures.

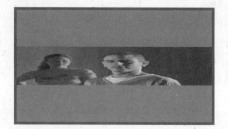

25

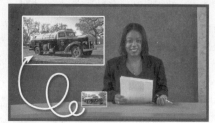

26

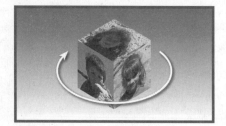

27

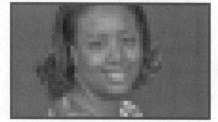

28

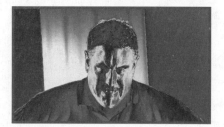

29

a. horizontal stretching

b. fly effect

c. solarization

d. mosaic effect

e. cube effect

REVIEW QUIZ

Mark the following statements as true or false by filling in the bubbles in the
T *(for true) or* **F** *(for false) column.*

		T	F
1.	You can use a green backdrop for chroma keying.	1 ○ 30	○ 31
2.	The titles for a normal, or luminance, key must have a strong brightness contrast with the background.	2 ○ 32	○ 33
3.	When chroma keying with a blue backdrop, the person who is to be keyed must wear blue.	3 ○ 34	○ 35
4.	When matching color energies, we are especially concerned about color harmony.	4 ○ 36	○ 37
5.	You can achieve a split-screen effect by stopping a horizontal wipe midway.	5 ○ 38	○ 39
6.	Before the C.G. can be used for a title, you must print the title on a studio card.	6 ○ 40	○ 41
7.	Filling keyed letters with a specific color is called a matte key.	7 ○ 42	○ 43
8.	Horizontal and vertical stretching can be done only with a digital signal.	8 ○ 44	○ 45
9.	In DTV you don't have to worry about the essential area.	9 ○ 46	○ 47
10.	Show titles should be appropriate to the style of the program.	10 ○ 48	○ 49
11.	A fly effect is possible only with DVE.	11 ○ 50	○ 51
12.	The aspect ratio of STV is 9 × 6.	12 ○ 52	○ 53
13.	In the fly mode, the image can zoom only from small to large.	13 ○ 54	○ 55
14.	A cube spin cannot be accomplished with an analog switcher.	14 ○ 56	○ 57
15.	The entire essential area must be filled with an image to show up on the TV screen.	15 ○ 58	○ 59
16.	Readability becomes an issue especially when the background is quite busy.	16 ○ 60	○ 61
17.	The ESS system functions like a large slide library and superfast slide projector.	17 ○ 62	○ 63
18.	The aspect ratio of HDTV is 16 × 9.	18 ○ 64	○ 65
19.	A mosaic effect can be achieved with an analog special-effects generator.	19 ○ 66	○ 67
20.	A superimposition has the foreground image block out portions of the background image as though the foreground image were cut into the background image.	20 ○ 68	○ 69

SECTION TOTAL [   ]

PROBLEM-SOLVING APPLICATIONS

1. The AD informs you that a dancer, who is supposed to be chroma-keyed over a videotaped landscape scene, is wearing a saturated blue leotard. The floor manager is very concerned about this news, but the PA assures you that the TD has already taken care of the problem. What was the potential problem? What could the TD do to solve it?

2. The preview monitor shows that the outline mode title key is hard to read over the busy background. How could you make the title more readable without changing either the font or the background?

3. You are the director of a new international interview show. Although the guests do not normally come to the studio personally but participate in the interview via satellite hookup, you nevertheless want each guest, when interviewed, to appear on the same screen with the interviewer. The TD tells you that this cannot be done because the switcher is not equipped with DVE equipment. What is your response?

4. Your client wants you to have his new line of automobiles rotate on a cube. How could you meet his request? What equipment would you need?

5. The producer of a documentary on the homeless asks the C.G. operator to redesign the titles because they are not befitting the style of the show. What does she mean? Give examples.

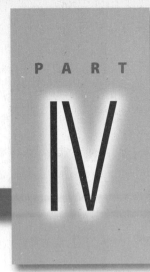

Image Control:
Switching, Recording,
and Editing

10 Switcher and Switching

REVIEW OF KEY TERMS

Match each term with its appropriate definition by filling in the corresponding bubble.

1. program bus
2. mix buses
3. key bus
4. preview/preset bus
5. fader bar
6. downstream keyer
7. switching
8. line-out
9. switcher

A. Rows of buttons that permit a super.

A ○ ○ ○ ○ ○
　 1　2　3　4　5
　 ○ ○ ○ ○
　 6　7　8　9

B. The bus (row of buttons) on the switcher, with inputs that are directly switched to the line-out.

B ○ ○ ○ ○ ○
　 1　2　3　4　5
　 ○ ○ ○ ○
　 6　7　8　9

C. A panel with rows of buttons that allows the selection and the assembly of various video sources.

C ○ ○ ○ ○ ○
　 1　2　3　4　5
　 ○ ○ ○ ○
　 6　7　8　9

D. A change from one video source to another and the creation of various transitions during the production.

D ○ ○ ○ ○ ○
　 1　2　3　4　5
　 ○ ○ ○ ○
　 6　7　8　9

E. A lever on the switcher that produces transitions and effects of different speeds.

E ○ ○ ○ ○ ○
　 1　2　3　4　5
　 ○ ○ ○ ○
　 6　7　8　9

PAGE
TOTAL ☐

1. program bus	4. preview/preset bus	7. switching
2. mix buses	5. fader bar	8. line-out
3. key bus	6. downstream keyer	9. switcher

F. A control that allows captions to be keyed over the picture (line-out signal) as it leaves the switcher.

F ○ ○ ○ ○ ○
   1 2 3 4 5
   ○ ○ ○ ○
   6 7 8 9

G. A row of buttons to select the video source to be inserted into the background image.

G ○ ○ ○ ○ ○
   1 2 3 4 5
   ○ ○ ○ ○
   6 7 8 9

H. A row of buttons that can direct an input to the preview/preset monitor.

H ○ ○ ○ ○ ○
   1 2 3 4 5
   ○ ○ ○ ○
   6 7 8 9

I. Carries the final video and audio signal to the video recorder or transmitter.

I ○ ○ ○ ○ ○
   1 2 3 4 5
   ○ ○ ○ ○
   6 7 8 9

PAGE TOTAL [ ]

SECTION TOTAL [ ]

REVIEW OF BASIC SWITCHER OPERATION

1. Fill in the bubbles whose numbers correspond with the appropriate parts of the switcher shown in the following figure.

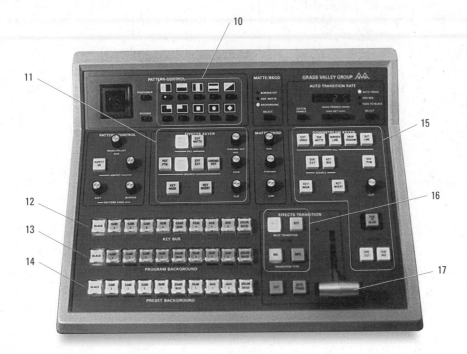

a. program bus

b. preset bus

c. fader bar

d. key bus

1a ○ ○ ○ ○
　　 10　11　12　13
　　 ○ ○ ○ ○
　　 14　15　16　17

1b ○ ○ ○ ○
　　 10　11　12　13
　　 ○ ○ ○ ○
　　 14　15　16　17

1c ○ ○ ○ ○
　　 10　11　12　13
　　 ○ ○ ○ ○
　　 14　15　16　17

1d ○ ○ ○ ○
　　 10　11　12　13
　　 ○ ○ ○ ○
　　 14　15　16　17

PAGE
TOTAL _____

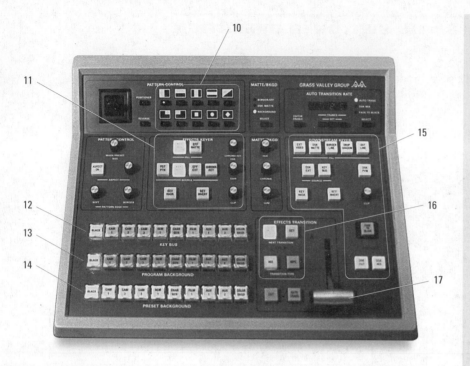

e. delegation controls (mix, wipe, key)

f. wipe pattern selector

g. downstream keyer controls

h. key/matte controls

2. Assuming that the switcher diagrams below are portions of a real switcher, you will see that several buttons have already been pressed. Some are high tally (fully lighted); others are low tally (dimly lighted). C1 is shooting a close-up of the newscaster, and C2 is framing a three-shot of the in-studio guests. (See monitor images below.) Select the correct monitor pair you would expect to see from the switcher output by filling in the corresponding bubbles.

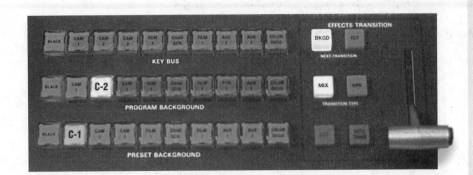

18

Preview

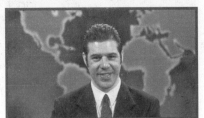

Line

19

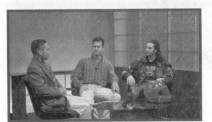

Preview

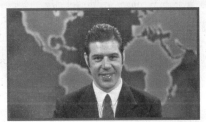

Line

20

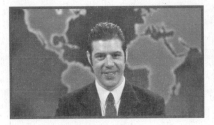

Preview

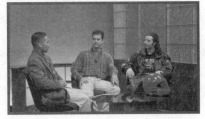

Line

PAGE TOTAL

Chapter 10 — *Switcher and Switching*

3. Select the correct monitor pair you would expect to see from the switcher output by filling in the corresponding bubbles.

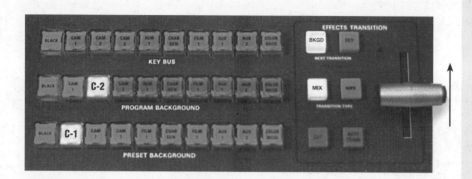

21
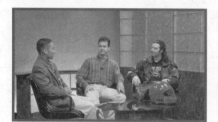

Preview

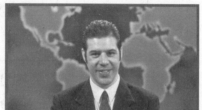

Line

22
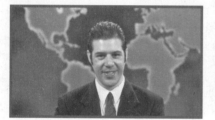

Preview

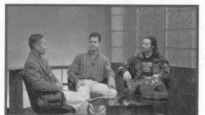

Line

23
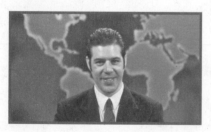

Preview

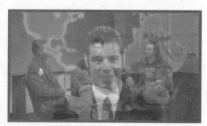

Line

Select the correct answers and fill in the bubbles with the corresponding numbers.

4. The program bus will direct the selected video source to the (24) *preview monitor* (25) *mix bus* (26) *line-out.*

4 ○ ○ ○
24 25 26

5. Assuming that camera 1 is on the air, you can cut to the VTR by pressing the (27) *KEY button* (28) *CUT button* (29) *VTR button* on the program bus.

5 ○ ○ ○
27 28 29

6. To select the functions of a specific bus or buses, you need to activate the (30) *downstream keyer* (31) *wipe pattern selector* (32) *specific delegation controls.*

6 ○ ○ ○
30 31 32

7. The highlighted buttons on the switcher below (Grass Valley 100) have already been pressed. To achieve a horizontal wipe from camera 1 to VTR 2, you still need to (33) *press the CUT button* (34) *press the key delegation control* (35) *move the fader bar to the opposite position or press the AUTO TRANS button.*

7 ○ ○ ○
33 34 35

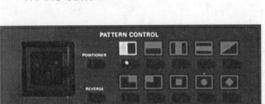

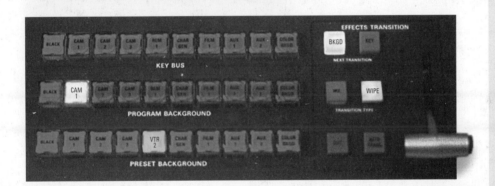

8. Assuming that you are working with a Grass Valley 100 switcher, you press the (36) *DSK and CUT* (37) *BKGD and MIX* (38) *KEY and WIPE* buttons to activate the mix function of the preset and program buses.

8 ○ ○ ○
36 37 38

9. To put the screen to black when the title was keyed with the DSK, you need to press the (39) *BLK button on the program bus* (40) *BLK button on the key bus* (41) *BLK button in the downstream keyer section.*

9 ○ ○ ○
39 40 41

PAGE
TOTAL [ ]

SECTION
TOTAL [ ]

Chapter 10 — Switcher and Switching

Mark the following statements as true or false by filling in the bubbles in the **T** (for true) or **F** (for false) column.

		T	F
1.	The length of the dissolve depends on how fast you move the fader bar from one end of travel to the other.	**1** ○ 42	○ 43
2.	The *AUTO TRANS* button on a switcher fulfills the same function as the fader bar.	**2** ○ 44	○ 45
3.	With a downstream keyer, you can add another title to one already created by the regular key bus before punching up both on the air.	**3** ○ 46	○ 47
4.	Everything punched up on the key bus will go directly to the line-out.	**4** ○ 48	○ 49
5.	You can assign the key bus a mix function.	**5** ○ 50	○ 51
6.	The switcher has a separate button for each input.	**6** ○ 52	○ 53
7.	If so delegated, the preview bus can become one of the mix buses.	**7** ○ 54	○ 55
8.	The key is one of the more useful transitions.	**8** ○ 56	○ 57
9.	When pushing the *BLK* button on the program bus, the line-out monitor goes to black even if the credits were generated by the downstream keyer.	**9** ○ 58	○ 59
10.	You can switch a cuts-only program entirely on the program bus.	**10** ○ 60	○ 61
11.	The program bus on a switcher sends the selected source directly to the line-out.	**11** ○ 62	○ 63
12.	If so delegated, the program bus can become the key bus.	**12** ○ 64	○ 65

SECTION TOTAL [   ]

PROBLEM-SOLVING APPLICATIONS

1. The director asks you, the TD, to superimpose a long shot of a dancer over a close-up of her face. First the director wants to have the long shot as the more prominent image and then slowly shift the emphasis in the super to the close-up. How, if at all, can you accomplish such an effect?

2. The director would like to have the total scene reveal itself gradually as though we were looking through a progressively expanding rectangle. She asks you to have the small rectangle start in the center of the screen with the proper TV aspect ratio and then expand to the full-size television screen. How, if at all, could you achieve this effect?

3. The producer would like to have an old-fashioned "The End" supered over the final shot of a chroma-keyed patio setting. He asks you, the TD, whether you can meet his request. How, if at all, could you achieve this effect?

4. In the multicamera, live-on-tape presentation of a highly precise balletlike dance piece, the director would like to use dissolves of exactly the same speed for all transitions. Can you do this? If so, how?

5. The same director would like to have several extremely quick cutting sequences during the argument scene between the prosecution and defense attorneys. She plans to cover the argument in tight cross-shots. How would you set up the switcher for these sequences?

 # Video Recording

REVIEW OF KEY TERMS

Match each term with its appropriate definition by filling in the corresponding bubble.

1. audio track
2. video track
3. analog VTR system
4. Y/C component video
5. composite video
6. multimedia
7. record protection
8. interactive video
9. nonlinear storage system
10. TBC
11. digital VTR system
12. control track
13. Y/color difference component video
14. NTSC
15. flash memory device
16. video server

A. The area of the videotape used for recording the audio information.

A
○ ○ ○ ○
1 2 3 4
○ ○ ○ ○
5 6 7 8
○ ○ ○ ○
9 10 11 12
○ ○ ○ ○
13 14 15 16

B. A videotape system that records video as a continuous signal.

B
○ ○ ○ ○
1 2 3 4
○ ○ ○ ○
5 6 7 8
○ ○ ○ ○
9 10 11 12
○ ○ ○ ○
13 14 15 16

PAGE
TOTAL ☐

© 2007 Thomson Wadsworth

1. audio track	7. record protection	12. control track
2. video track	8. interactive video	13. Y/color difference
3. analog VTR system	9. nonlinear storage	component video
4. Y/C component video	system	14. NTSC
5. composite video	10. TBC	15. flash memory device
6. multimedia	11. digital VTR system	16. video server

C. The area of the videotape used for recording the video information.

C
○ ○ ○ ○
1 2 3 4
○ ○ ○ ○
5 6 7 8
○ ○ ○ ○
9 10 11 12
○ ○ ○ ○
13 14 15 16

D. A device that makes videotape edits and playback more stable.

D
○ ○ ○ ○
1 2 3 4
○ ○ ○ ○
5 6 7 8
○ ○ ○ ○
9 10 11 12
○ ○ ○ ○
13 14 15 16

E. A read/write digital storage medium of limited capacity.

E
○ ○ ○ ○
1 2 3 4
○ ○ ○ ○
5 6 7 8
○ ○ ○ ○
9 10 11 12
○ ○ ○ ○
13 14 15 16

F. A system that combines the Y (black-and-white) and C (red, green, and blue) video information into a single signal.

F
○ ○ ○ ○
1 2 3 4
○ ○ ○ ○
5 6 7 8
○ ○ ○ ○
9 10 11 12
○ ○ ○ ○
13 14 15 16

PAGE
TOTAL

1. audio track	7. record protection	12. control track
2. video track	8. interactive video	13. Y/color difference
3. analog VTR system	9. nonlinear storage	component video
4. Y/C component video	system	14. NTSC
5. composite video	10. TBC	15. flash memory device
6. multimedia	11. digital VTR system	16. video server

G. A device on the videocassette that prevents accidental erasure.

G
○ ○ ○ ○
1 2 3 4
○ ○ ○ ○
5 6 7 8
○ ○ ○ ○
9 10 11 12
○ ○ ○ ○
13 14 15 16

H. A system that separates the Y and C signals and treats the luminance and color as separate signals but combines them during the recording.

H
○ ○ ○ ○
1 2 3 4
○ ○ ○ ○
5 6 7 8
○ ○ ○ ○
9 10 11 12
○ ○ ○ ○
13 14 15 16

I. A system that keeps the Y and C signals separate throughout the video-recording process.

I
○ ○ ○ ○
1 2 3 4
○ ○ ○ ○
5 6 7 8
○ ○ ○ ○
9 10 11 12
○ ○ ○ ○
13 14 15 16

J. The simultaneous computer display of text, still and moving images, and sound. Usually recorded on CD-ROM.

J
○ ○ ○ ○
1 2 3 4
○ ○ ○ ○
5 6 7 8
○ ○ ○ ○
9 10 11 12
○ ○ ○ ○
13 14 15 16

P A G E
T O T A L [   ]

1.	audio track	7.	record protection	12.	control track
2.	video track	8.	interactive video	13.	Y/color difference
3.	analog VTR system	9.	nonlinear storage		component video
4.	Y/C component video		system	14.	NTSC
5.	composite video	10.	TBC	15.	flash memory device
6.	multimedia	11.	digital VTR system	16.	video server

K. Storage of video and audio material in digital form on a hard drive or read/write optical disc. Each frame can be accessed by the computer independent of all others.

K
○ ○ ○ ○
1 2 3 4
○ ○ ○ ○
5 6 7 8
○ ○ ○ ○
9 10 11 12
○ ○ ○ ○
13 14 15 16

L. A computer-driven video program that gives the viewer some control over what to see and how to see it. It is often used as a training device.

L
○ ○ ○ ○
1 2 3 4
○ ○ ○ ○
5 6 7 8
○ ○ ○ ○
9 10 11 12
○ ○ ○ ○
13 14 15 16

M. Stands for National Television System Committee. Designates the composite signal system.

M
○ ○ ○ ○
1 2 3 4
○ ○ ○ ○
5 6 7 8
○ ○ ○ ○
9 10 11 12
○ ○ ○ ○
13 14 15 16

N. The track that contains the sync pulses.

N
○ ○ ○ ○
1 2 3 4
○ ○ ○ ○
5 6 7 8
○ ○ ○ ○
9 10 11 12
○ ○ ○ ○
13 14 15 16

PAGE TOTAL [   ]

1. audio track	7. record protection	12. control track
2. video track	8. interactive video	13. Y/color difference
3. analog VTR system	9. nonlinear storage	component video
4. Y/C component video	system	14. NTSC
5. composite video	10. TBC	15. flash memory device
6. multimedia	11. digital VTR system	16. video server

O. A videotape system that records video as a series of on/off pulses.

P. A high-capacity hard drive for storage and playback of video programs.

O
○ ○ ○ ○
1 2 3 4
○ ○ ○ ○
5 6 7 8
○ ○ ○ ○
9 10 11 12
○ ○ ○ ○
13 14 15 16

P
○ ○ ○ ○
1 2 3 4
○ ○ ○ ○
5 6 7 8
○ ○ ○ ○
9 10 11 12
○ ○ ○ ○
13 14 15 16

PAGE TOTAL
SECTION TOTAL

REVIEW OF VIDEOTAPE RECORDING SYSTEMS

Select the correct answers and fill in the bubbles with the corresponding numbers.

1. The NTSC signal is (17) *composite* (18) *component*.

1	○ 17	○ 18

2. The Y/color difference signal is (19) *composite* (20) *component*.

2	○ 19	○ 20

3. The Y/C system is (21) *composite* (22) *component*.

3	○ 21	○ 22

4. To keep the quality loss to a minimum during extensive postproduction editing, you should use (23) *analog* (24) *digital* VTRs and a (25) *composite* (26) *component* system. *(Fill in two bubbles.)*

4	○ 23	○ 24
	○ 25	○ 26

5. All ½-inch VTR formats are (27) *compatible* (28) *not compatible* and, therefore, (29) *can* (30) *cannot* all be played back on a regular VHS videotape machine. *(Fill in two bubbles.)*

5	○ 27	○ 28
	○ 29	○ 30

6. You (31) *can* (32) *cannot* play a regular VHS tape on an S-VHS recorder, but you (33) *can* (34) *cannot* play an S-VHS tape on a regular VHS recorder. *(Fill in two bubbles.)*

6	○ 31	○ 32
	○ 33	○ 34

7. DVCAM and DVCPRO systems are (35) *compatible* (36) *not compatible,* which means that you (37) *can* (38) *cannot* play back a DVCPRO tape on a standard DVCAM machine and vice versa. *(Fill in two bubbles.)*

7	○ 35	○ 36
	○ 37	○ 38

8. A flash memory device has (39) *an optical disc drive* (40) *a hard disk drive* (41) *no moving parts*.

8	○ 39	○ 40	○ 41

9. Videotape can record (42) *digital information only* (43) *analog information only* (44) *both digital and analog information*.

9	○ 42	○ 43	○ 44

SECTION TOTAL ▢

REVIEW OF THE VIDEO-RECORDING PROCESS

Select the correct answers and fill in the bubbles with the corresponding numbers.

1. To record on a videocassette, the protection tab must be in the (45) *open* (46) *closed* position, or (47) *broken off* (48) *unbroken*. ***(Fill in two bubbles.)***

1	○ 45	○ 46
	○ 47	○ 48

2. Color bars are useful only when they are (49) *generated by the equipment you are actually using* (50) *dubbed from a color bar master tape* (51) *digitally generated.*

2	○ 49	○ 50	○ 51

3. Mark the items that are part of a normal video leader: (52) *color bars* (53) *identification slate* (54) *control track display* (55) *test tone* (56) *edit decision list* (57) *video test pattern.* ***(Multiple answers are possible.)***

3	○ 52	○ 53	○ 54
	○ 55	○ 56	○ 57

4. The most common video connectors are (58) *XLR* (59) *mini plug* (60) *BNC* (61) *RCA phono.* ***(Multiple answers are possible.)***

4	○ 58	○ 59	○ 60	○ 61

SECTION TOTAL [   ]

REVIEW OF NONLINEAR STORAGE SYSTEMS

Select the correct answers and fill in the bubbles with the corresponding numbers.

1. Of the following, the "read-only" digital storage device is a (62) *flash drive* (63) *hard drive* (64) *digital VTR* (65) *standard CD-ROM.*

1	○ 62	○ 63	○ 64	○ 65

2. Indicate which of the following video storage devices is linear: (66) *DVD* (67) *hard drive* (68) *videotape* (69) *video server.*

2	○ 66	○ 67	○ 68	○ 69

3. The ESS system can grab and digitize a video frame (70) *only from a digital videotape* (71) *only from an analog videotape* (72) *from any video source.*

3	○ 70	○ 71	○ 72

4. Digital videotape recordings are (73) *linear* (74) *nonlinear* and (75) *allow* (76) *do not allow* random access. ***(Fill in two bubbles.)***

4	○ 73	○ 74
	○ 75	○ 76

5. The optical storage device that you can erase and reuse for a new recording of video and audio information is a (77) *CD-R* (78) *DVD* (79) *DVD-RW.*

5	○ 77	○ 78	○ 79

SECTION TOTAL [   ]

REVIEW QUIZ

Mark the following statements as true or false by filling in the bubbles in the **T** *(for true) or* **F** *(for false) column.*

		T	F
1.	In a Y/color difference component system, the primary color signals are kept separate throughout the recording process.	1 ○ 80	○ 81
2.	The Y/C component system means that the color yellow has been added to the color signals.	2 ○ 82	○ 83
3.	*NTSC signal* and *composite signal* mean the same thing.	3 ○ 84	○ 85
4.	Color bars help in adjusting the colors on the playback monitor.	4 ○ 86	○ 87
5.	A video leader should always be dubbed over from a master recording of standard video leaders.	5 ○ 88	○ 89
6.	A TBC helps eliminate picture jitter.	6 ○ 90	○ 91
7.	You can play back a DVCAM videotape on an S-VHS recorder.	7 ○ 92	○ 93
8.	You can play back a VHS videotape on an S-VHS recorder.	8 ○ 94	○ 95
9.	The difference between DVCPRO and DVCAM systems is that the DVCPRO system is digital whereas the DVCAM system is analog.	9 ○ 96	○ 97
10.	All digital videotapes are linear storage devices.	10 ○ 98	○ 99
11.	The video leader includes a 0 VU test tone.	11 ○ 100	○ 101
12.	Dubbing analog videotape produces much more deterioration from one generation to the next than when dubbing digital videotape.	12 ○ 102	○ 103
13.	To record on a cassette, the tab must be intact or in the closed position.	13 ○ 104	○ 105
14.	Y/C component video and S-video are the same.	14 ○ 106	○ 107
15.	A flash drive can hold as much information as a standard mini-cassette.	15 ○ 108	○ 109

SECTION TOTAL

PROBLEM-SOLVING APPLICATIONS

1. Your assistant shows you the first draft of an entry form for a statewide video competition. The specifications for tape formats read as follows: "Only digital recording formats will be accepted." Will you recommend any changes to this form? If so, why? If not, why not?

2. The CEO of a video production company asks you whether DVCAM video-cassettes can be played back on his DVCPRO recorder. What is your reply?

3. You are asked by the new dean of the College of Communications whether to invest in digital camcorders that use videotape as the recording medium, or camcorders with tapeless recording systems, such as hard drives, optical discs, and flash memory devices. Which type of system would you recommend?

4. The same dean asks you about the difference between mini-cassettes and larger digital tape cassettes. What would you tell him?

5. The novice director tells you that you don't have to keep a field log because you will have to log the tapes anyway before editing. What is your reaction?

12 Postproduction: Linear and Nonlinear Editing

REVIEW OF KEY TERMS

Match each term with its appropriate definition by filling in the corresponding bubble.

1. **linear editing system**
2. **edit controller**
3. **NLE**
4. **SMPTE time code**
5. **pulse-count system**

6. **off-line editing**
7. **window dub**
8. **on-line editing**
9. **EDL**
10. **assemble editing**

11. **insert editing**
12. **capture**
13. **VTR log**
14. **rough-cut**

A. Produces the final high-quality edit master tape in linear editing and recaptures selected shots in high-resolution in nonlinear editing.

A ○ ○ ○ ○ ○
   1   2   3   4   5
   ○ ○ ○ ○ ○
   6   7   8   9   10
   ○ ○ ○ ○
   11 12 13 14

B. Uses videotape as the recording medium.

B ○ ○ ○ ○ ○
   1   2   3   4   5
   ○ ○ ○ ○ ○
   6   7   8   9   10
   ○ ○ ○ ○
   11 12 13 14

C. Consists of edit-in and edit-out cues, expressed in time code numbers, and the nature and transitions between shots.

C ○ ○ ○ ○ ○
   1   2   3   4   5
   ○ ○ ○ ○ ○
   6   7   8   9   10
   ○ ○ ○ ○
   11 12 13 14

PAGE TOTAL [ ]

© 2007 Thomson Wadsworth

1. linear editing system	6. off-line editing	11. insert editing
2. edit controller	7. window dub	12. capture
3. NLE	8. on-line editing	13. VTR log
4. SMPTE time code	9. EDL	14. rough-cut
5. pulse-count system	10. assemble editing	

D. A device that facilitates various editing functions, such as marking edit-in and edit-out points.

D ○ ○ ○ ○ ○
   1 2 3 4 5
   ○ ○ ○ ○ ○
   6 7 8 9 10
   ○ ○ ○ ○
   11 12 13 14

E. The capture of shots in low resolution or an editing process that is not intended for producing an edit master.

E ○ ○ ○ ○ ○
   1 2 3 4 5
   ○ ○ ○ ○ ○
   6 7 8 9 10
   ○ ○ ○ ○
   11 12 13 14

F. A popular address code that marks each video frame with a specific number.

F ○ ○ ○ ○ ○
   1 2 3 4 5
   ○ ○ ○ ○ ○
   6 7 8 9 10
   ○ ○ ○ ○
   11 12 13 14

G. Another name for a preliminary off-line edit.

G ○ ○ ○ ○ ○
   1 2 3 4 5
   ○ ○ ○ ○ ○
   6 7 8 9 10
   ○ ○ ○ ○
   11 12 13 14

H. The transfer of a camcorder video to the hard drive of a computer.

H ○ ○ ○ ○ ○
   1 2 3 4 5
   ○ ○ ○ ○ ○
   6 7 8 9 10
   ○ ○ ○ ○
   11 12 13 14

I. The list of all takes on the source tapes used for editing. May have vector notations.

I ○ ○ ○ ○ ○
   1 2 3 4 5
   ○ ○ ○ ○ ○
   6 7 8 9 10
   ○ ○ ○ ○
   11 12 13 14

P A G E
T O T A L [   ]

1. linear editing system	6. off-line editing	11. insert editing
2. edit controller	7. window dub	12. capture
3. NLE	8. on-line editing	13. VTR log
4. SMPTE time code	9. EDL	14. rough-cut
5. pulse-count system	10. assemble editing	

J. An address code that uses the control track pulses to count elapsed time and frame numbers.

J ○ ○ ○ ○ ○
  1 2 3 4 5
  ○ ○ ○ ○ ○
  6 7 8 9 10
  ○ ○ ○ ○
  11 12 13 14

K. Produces highly stable edits. Requires prior laying of control track on edit master tape.

K ○ ○ ○ ○ ○
  1 2 3 4 5
  ○ ○ ○ ○ ○
  6 7 8 9 10
  ○ ○ ○ ○
  11 12 13 14

L. Adding shots on the edit master tape without the prior recording of a control track.

L ○ ○ ○ ○ ○
  1 2 3 4 5
  ○ ○ ○ ○ ○
  6 7 8 9 10
  ○ ○ ○ ○
  11 12 13 14

M. Allows random access of shots. The video and audio information is stored in digital form on computer disks.

M ○ ○ ○ ○ ○
  1 2 3 4 5
  ○ ○ ○ ○ ○
  6 7 8 9 10
  ○ ○ ○ ○
  11 12 13 14

N. A copy of the source tapes to a lower-quality tape format with the address code keyed into each frame.

N ○ ○ ○ ○ ○
  1 2 3 4 5
  ○ ○ ○ ○ ○
  6 7 8 9 10
  ○ ○ ○ ○
  11 12 13 14

PAGE TOTAL [   ]

SECTION TOTAL [   ]

Select the correct answers and fill in the bubbles with the corresponding numbers.

1. With a nonlinear system, you can create (15) *cuts only* (16) *cuts and dissolves only* (17) *a great number of special transition effects.*

   | 1 | ◯ 15 | ◯ 16 | ◯ 17 |

2. Because in the insert editing mode the record VTR (18) *will* (19) *will not* transfer the control track of the source tape, you (20) *need* (21) *do not need* to prerecord a continuous control track on the edit master tape. **(Fill in two bubbles.)**

   | 2 | ◯ 18 | ◯ 19 |
   | | ◯ 20 | ◯ 21 |

3. When editing video and audio separately with a linear system, you need to be in the (22) *assemble* (23) *audio* (24) *insert* mode.

   | 3 | ◯ 22 | ◯ 23 | ◯ 24 |

4. A successful capture requires that the analog source tapes are first (25) *digitized* (26) *window-dubbed* (27) *blackened.*

   | 4 | ◯ 25 | ◯ 26 | ◯ 27 |

5. The pulse-count editing system is (28) *more accurate* (29) *less accurate* in locating a specific frame than the time code system because it (30) *marks* (31) *does not mark* each individual frame with a specific address. **(Fill in two bubbles.)**

   | 5 | ◯ 28 | ◯ 29 |
   | | ◯ 30 | ◯ 31 |

6. Linear systems (32) *allow* (33) *do not allow* random access to the source material, and use (34) *videotape* (35) *computer disks* for their source material. **(Fill in two bubbles.)**

   | 6 | ◯ 32 | ◯ 33 |
   | | ◯ 34 | ◯ 35 |

7. When in the assemble mode, you (36) *must prelay the control track on the edit master tape before editing* (37) *stripe all source tapes with a control track* (38) *simply copy the selected shots onto the edit master tape.*

   | 7 | ◯ 36 | ◯ 37 | ◯ 38 |

8. When using a normal linear single-source editing system, you can perform (39) *cuts and dissolves* (40) *cuts and wipes* (41) *wipes only* (42) *cuts only.*

   | 8 | ◯ 39 | ◯ 40 | ◯ 41 | ◯ 42 |

9. Contrary to linear systems, nonlinear systems allow (43) *random* (44) *nonrandom* (45) *sequential* access to each frame.

   | 9 | ◯ 43 | ◯ 44 | ◯ 45 |

10. Fill in the bubbles whose numbers correspond with the numbers identifying the EDL mistakes in the following figure:

    | 10 | ◯ 46 | ◯ 47 | ◯ 48 |
    | | ◯ 49 | ◯ 50 | ◯ 51 |

IN	OUT	
01 : 17 : 28 : 29	01 : 17 : 28 : 45	46
01 : 17 : 30 : 15	01 : 17 : 45 : 01	47
01 : 19 : 15 : 29	01 : 19 : 14 : 07	48
01 : 21 : 65 : 33	01 : 32 : 59 : 29	49
02 : 17 : 28 : 15	02 : 18 : 37 : 06	50
02 : 17 : 29 : 16	01 : 18 : 45 : 29	51

SECTION TOTAL

REVIEW QUIZ

Mark the following statements as true or false by filling in the bubbles in the
T *(for true) or* ***F*** *(for false) column.*

		T	F
1.	The edit controller for a linear editing system facilitates random access of various shots.	**1** ○ 52	○ 53
2.	Time code must be recorded with the actual production to achieve a continuous frame address.	**2** ○ 54	○ 55
3.	Once the source tapes are captured, nonlinear editing systems do not use source VTRs.	**3** ○ 56	○ 57
4.	The expanded linear editing system needs at least two source VTRs.	**4** ○ 58	○ 59
5.	In linear editing you must be in the insert mode to split audio and video.	**5** ○ 60	○ 61
6.	The pulse-count system marks each frame with a unique address.	**6** ○ 62	○ 63
7.	All analog source tapes must be digitized before audio and video information can be stored on the NLE hard drive.	**7** ○ 64	○ 65
8.	An EDL is necessary only if you do nonlinear editing.	**8** ○ 66	○ 67
9.	The SMPTE time code marks each frame with a unique address.	**9** ○ 68	○ 69
10.	A window dub keys a specific time code address over each frame.	**10** ○ 70	○ 71
11.	Ordinarily, off-line editing does not produce the final edit master tape.	**11** ○ 72	○ 73
12.	Nonlinear editing systems allow random access to pictures and sound.	**12** ○ 74	○ 75
13.	Nonlinear systems do not need a time code.	**13** ○ 76	○ 77
14.	The basic principle of nonlinear editing is file management rather than tape copying.	**14** ○ 78	○ 79
15.	You don't need two source VTRs to create a dissolve with an NLE system.	**15** ○ 80	○ 81
16.	You should use insert editing only when replacing a shot in an edit master tape.	**16** ○ 82	○ 83
17.	In nonlinear editing, the source tape video as well as the audio must be stored on a computer storage device.	**17** ○ 84	○ 85

SECTION TOTAL ☐

1. You are asked by the corporate manager to justify the purchase of a nonlinear editing system for the company's daily news show. What will be your major points?

2. The same corporate manager tells you that he has denied your request for a portable linear editing system for your overseas news coverage because your digital cameras require a nonlinear system. Do you agree or disagree with the manager. Why?

3. You are told to skip the off-line editing step because the desktop editing system will produce a high-quality edit master anyway. What is your comment?

4. The director is not concerned about continuity or cutaways during the shooting phase because the nonlinear editing system makes it easy to fix continuity problems. What is your reaction? Be specific.

5. You are told that you can skip making a window dub when using an NLE system because each frame will show a time code readout on the computer screen anyhow. What is your reaction?

13 Editing Principles

REVIEW OF KEY TERMS

Match each term with its appropriate definition by filling in the corresponding bubble.

1. continuity editing
2. complexity editing
3. continuing vectors
4. mental map

5. diverging vectors
6. jump cut
7. converging vectors
8. vector line

9. jogging
10. cutaway

A. An imaginary line created by extending converging index vectors, or the direction of a motion vector.

A ○ ○ ○ ○ ○
   1 2 3 4 5
   ○ ○ ○ ○ ○
   6 7 8 9 10

B. An image that jerks slightly from one screen position to another during a cut.

B ○ ○ ○ ○ ○
   1 2 3 4 5
   ○ ○ ○ ○ ○
   6 7 8 9 10

C. Index and motion vectors that point away from each other.

C ○ ○ ○ ○ ○
   1 2 3 4 5
   ○ ○ ○ ○ ○
   6 7 8 9 10

D. Index and motion vectors that point toward each other.

D ○ ○ ○ ○ ○
   1 2 3 4 5
   ○ ○ ○ ○ ○
   6 7 8 9 10

E. Tells us where things are or are supposed to be on- and off-screen.

E ○ ○ ○ ○ ○
   1 2 3 4 5
   ○ ○ ○ ○ ○
   6 7 8 9 10

PAGE TOTAL [   ]

© 2007 Thomson Wadsworth

1. continuity editing	5. diverging vectors	9. jogging
2. complexity editing	6. jump cut	10. cutaway
3. continuing vectors	7. converging vectors	
4. mental map	8. vector line	

F. The building of an intensified screen event from carefully selected and juxtaposed shots.

F ○ ○ ○ ○ ○
   1   2   3   4   5
○ ○ ○ ○ ○
6   7   8   9   10

G. Graphic vectors that extend each other, or index and motion vectors pointing and moving in the same direction.

G ○ ○ ○ ○ ○
   1   2   3   4   5
○ ○ ○ ○ ○
6   7   8   9   10

H. The assembly of shots to ensure vector continuity.

H ○ ○ ○ ○ ○
   1   2   3   4   5
○ ○ ○ ○ ○
6   7   8   9   10

I. Frame-by-frame advancement of videotape, resulting in jerky motion.

I ○ ○ ○ ○ ○
   1   2   3   4   5
○ ○ ○ ○ ○
6   7   8   9   10

J. A shot that is used to intercut between two shots in which the screen direction is reversed.

J ○ ○ ○ ○ ○
   1   2   3   4   5
○ ○ ○ ○ ○
6   7   8   9   10

P A G E
T O T A L

SECTION
TOTAL

REVIEW OF AESTHETIC PRINCIPLES OF CONTINUITY EDITING

Select the correct answers and fill in the bubbles with the corresponding numbers.

1. A jump cut means that the subject is (11) *jumping up and down* (12) *causing the videotape to break up at the edit point* (13) *perceived as abruptly changing from one screen position to the next.*

1 ◯ ◯ ◯
    11   12   13

2. Vectors indicate (14) *a direction* (15) *an edit command* (16) *a specific address code.*

2 ◯ ◯ ◯
    14   15   16

3. To preserve index vector continuity, you (17) *must cross the vector line* (18) *should not cross the vector line* (19) *should ignore the vector line.*

3 ◯ ◯ ◯
    17   18   19

4. In continuity editing you are primarily concerned with maintaining (20) *story continuity* (21) *schedule efficiency* (22) *vector continuity.*

4 ◯ ◯ ◯
    20   21   22

5. To preserve motion vector continuity, you (23) *must cross the vector line* (24) *should not cross the vector line* (25) *should ignore the vector line.*

5 ◯ ◯ ◯
    23   24   25

6. To preserve graphic vector continuity, observing the vector line is (26) *essential* (27) *recommended* (28) *irrelevant.*

6 ◯ ◯ ◯
    26   27   28

7. The mental map includes (29) *only on-screen positions and directions* (30) *only off-screen positions and directions* (31) *both on- and off-screen positions and directions.*

7 ◯ ◯ ◯
    29   30   31

8. In the following figures, select the camera that is in the *wrong* place for continuity editing and fill in the corresponding bubble. Draw the principal vector line on all the figures (a–d).

a. Over-the-shoulder shots of person A and person B.

8a ◯ ◯ ◯
     32   33   34

P A G E
T O T A L ☐

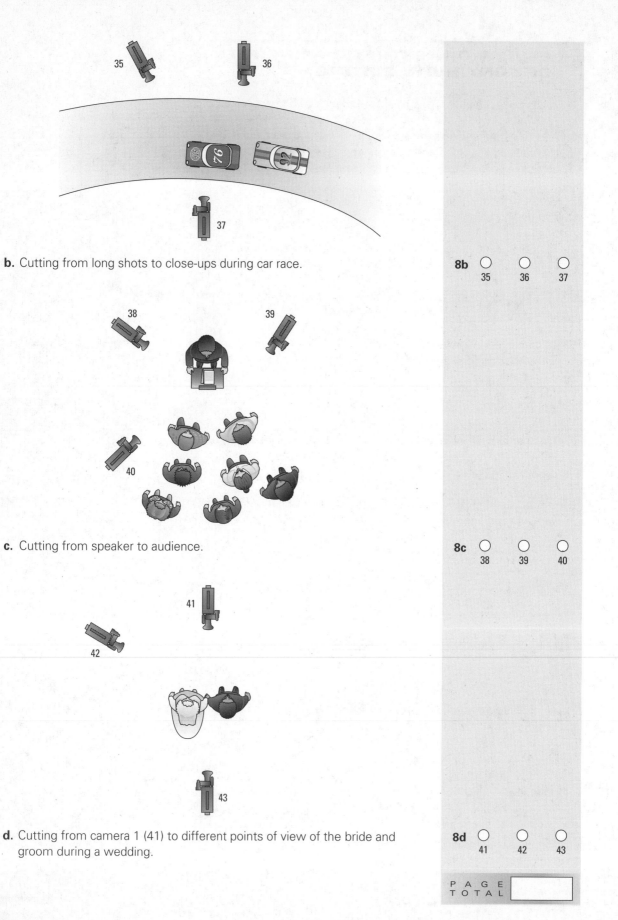

b. Cutting from long shots to close-ups during car race.

c. Cutting from speaker to audience.

d. Cutting from camera 1 (41) to different points of view of the bride and groom during a wedding.

9. For each of the following storyboard pairs, indicate whether the shots
(44) *can* (45) *cannot* be edited together to form converging index vectors.

a.

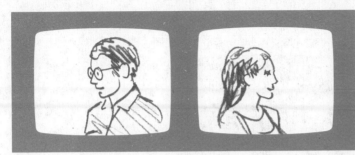

b.

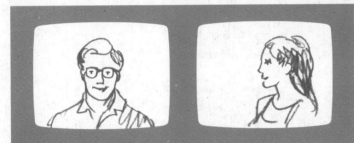

9b ◯ ◯
44 45

c.

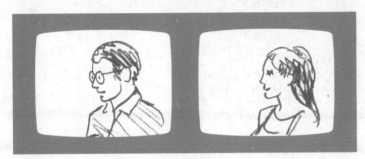

9c ◯ ◯
44 45

d.

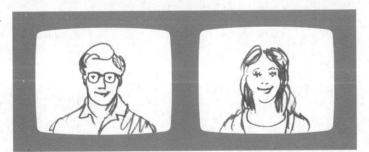

9d ◯ ◯
44 45

PAGE
TOTAL ▢

10. Cutting together the two shots shown below will result in (46) *a jump cut* (47) *diverging vectors* (48) *reversal of screen direction.*

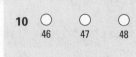

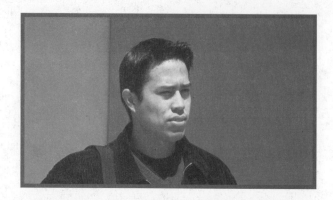

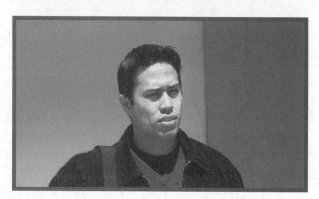

REVIEW QUIZ

Mark the following statements as true or false by filling in the bubbles in the **T** *(for true) or* **F** *(for false) column.*

		T	F
1.	When crossing the vector line during over-the-shoulder shooting, the talent will switch screen positions.	1 ○ 49	○ 50
2.	Complexity editing requires a much stricter observance of the vector line principle than does continuity editing.	2 ○ 51	○ 52
3.	The primary function of complexity editing is to maintain the viewer's mental map.	3 ○ 53	○ 54
4.	Motion vectors can be continuing or converging but not diverging.	4 ○ 55	○ 56
5.	Z-axis index vectors can be converging or diverging, depending on context.	5 ○ 57	○ 58
6.	Motion vectors cannot converge in a single shot.	6 ○ 59	○ 60
7.	The mental map includes on-screen as well as off-screen positions.	7 ○ 61	○ 62
8.	Postproduction editing is done primarily to fix production mistakes.	8 ○ 63	○ 64
9.	In complexity editing, a jump cut can be used to intensify the event.	9 ○ 65	○ 66
10.	The vector line is especially relevant for preserving screen positions and index and motion vector continuity.	10 ○ 67	○ 68

SECTION
TOTAL [   ]

© 2007 Thomson Wadsworth

PROBLEM-SOLVING APPLICATIONS

1. The new production intern suggests that you cover the New Year's parade by placing cameras exactly opposite each other on both sides of the street. How would you respond to the intern?

2. The host mispronounces the name of the guest during the videotaping of an interview. The director opts for going on rather than doing the opening again because "we can fix it in post." Do you agree with the director's decision? If so, why? If not, why not?

3. The director of a cable company production group tells you not to worry about what happens in off-screen space when editing because the "viewer" will not see what is going on in off-screen space anyway. What is your response?

4. A retired, highly experienced film director tells you to avoid jump cuts at all costs. What is your reaction?

5. When you want to cross the vector line with the camera to intensify a scene, the producer tells you that this is an absolute no-no. How would you justify "crossing the line"?

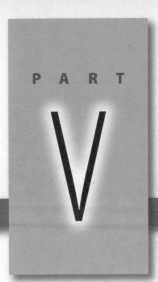

PART

V

Production Environment: Studio, Field, and Synthetic

14 Production Environment: The Studio

REVIEW OF KEY TERMS

Match each term with its appropriate definition by filling in the corresponding bubble.

1. cyclorama
2. P.L.
3. S.A.
4. intercom
5. studio control room
6. monitor
7. master control
8. flats
9. props
10. floor plan
11. I.F.B.

A. Major intercommunication device in video production studios.

A ① ② ③ ④ / 1 2 3 4
⑤ ⑥ ⑦ ⑧ / 5 6 7 8
⑨ ⑩ ⑪ / 9 10 11

B. A U-shaped continuous piece of canvas or muslin for backing of scenery and action.

B 1 2 3 4
5 6 7 8
9 10 11

C. Furniture and other objects used by talent and for set decoration.

C 1 2 3 4
5 6 7 8
9 10 11

PAGE TOTAL _____

© 2007 Thomson Wadsworth

1. cyclorama	5. studio control room	9. props
2. P.L.	6. monitor	10. floor plan
3. S.A.	7. master control	11. I.F.B.
4. intercom	8. flats	

D. A room adjacent to the studio in which the director, the producer, various production assistants, the TD (technical director), the audio engineer, and sometimes the LD (lighting director) perform their various production functions.

D
○ ○ ○ ○
1 2 3 4
○ ○ ○ ○
5 6 7 8
○ ○ ○
9 10 11

E. A diagram of scenery, properties, and set dressings drawn on a grid.

E
○ ○ ○ ○
1 2 3 4
○ ○ ○ ○
5 6 7 8
○ ○ ○
9 10 11

F. A public-address loudspeaker system from the control room to the studio.

F
○ ○ ○ ○
1 2 3 4
○ ○ ○ ○
5 6 7 8
○ ○ ○
9 10 11

G. High-quality video receiver used in the studio and control rooms. Cannot receive broadcast signals.

G
○ ○ ○ ○
1 2 3 4
○ ○ ○ ○
5 6 7 8
○ ○ ○
9 10 11

H. Allows the director to give the talent instructions while the talent is on the air.

H
○ ○ ○ ○
1 2 3 4
○ ○ ○ ○
5 6 7 8
○ ○ ○
9 10 11

PAGE
TOTAL

1. cyclorama	5. studio control room	9. props
2. P.L.	6. monitor	10. floor plan
3. S.A.	7. master control	11. I.F.B.
4. intercom	8. flats	

I. Communication system for all production and engineering personnel involved in the production of a show. Includes I.F.B., P.L., S.A., and cellular telephones.

I ○ ○ ○ ○
　1　2　3　4
○ ○ ○ ○
5　6　7　8
○ ○ ○
9　10　11

J. Pieces of standing scenery used as background or to simulate the walls of a room.

J ○ ○ ○ ○
　1　2　3　4
○ ○ ○ ○
5　6　7　8
○ ○ ○
9　10　11

K. Controls the program input, storage, and retrieval of on-the-air telecasts. Also oversees technical quality of all program material.

K ○ ○ ○ ○
　1　2　3　4
○ ○ ○ ○
5　6　7　8
○ ○ ○
9　10　11

PAGE TOTAL ☐

SECTION TOTAL ☐

REVIEW OF VIDEO PRODUCTION STUDIO AND MAJOR INSTALLATIONS

Select the correct answers and fill in the bubbles with the corresponding numbers.

1. Even for small studios, the minimum ceiling height is (12) *12 feet* (13) *14 feet* (14) *18 feet.*

2. The major function of a cyc is to serve as (15) *a sound-deadening device* (16) *continuous background for scenery* (17) *a chroma-key area.*

3. You need a separate video monitor (18) *for each video switcher input* (19) *for preset and line video only* (20) *for remote inputs only.*

4. The switcher should be located adjacent to the (21) *LD's* (22) *director's* (23) *producer's* (24) *C.G. operator's* position.

5. Assuming that the off-the-air receiver (AIR) shows the correct C.G. image, which preview monitors display the wrong picture? *(Multiple answers are possible.)*

(25) *VT-1 monitor*	(32) *line monitor*
(26) *VT-2 monitor*	(33) *C-1 monitor*
(27) *VT-3 monitor*	(34) *C-2 monitor*
(28) *character generator monitor*	(35) *C-3 monitor*
(29) *electronic still store monitor*	(36) *remote-1 monitor*
(30) *effects monitor*	(37) *remote-2 monitor*
(31) *preview monitor*	

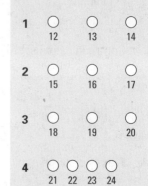

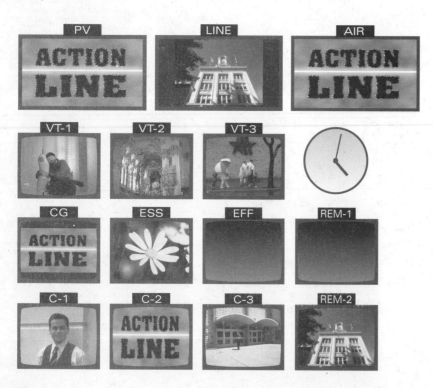

1 ○ 12   ○ 13   ○ 14

2 ○ 15   ○ 16   ○ 17

3 ○ 18   ○ 19   ○ 20

4 ○ 21 ○ 22 ○ 23 ○ 24

5 ○ 25 ○ 26 ○ 27 ○ 28 ○ 29
     ○ 30 ○ 31 ○ 32 ○ 33 ○ 34
     ○ 35 ○ 36 ○ 37

SECTION TOTAL ▢

REVIEW OF SCENERY, PROPERTIES, AND SCENIC DESIGN

1. Fill in the bubbles whose numbers correspond with the numbers identifying the various set pieces in the following figure.

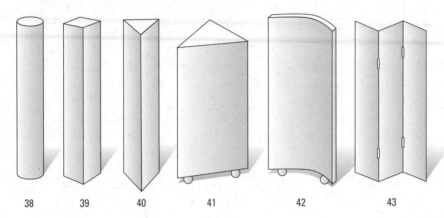

| 38 | 39 | 40 | 41 | 42 | 43 |

a. sweep

1a ○ 38 ○ 39 ○ 40
○ 41 ○ 42 ○ 43

b. periaktos

1b ○ 38 ○ 39 ○ 40
○ 41 ○ 42 ○ 43

c. pillar

1c ○ 38 ○ 39 ○ 40
○ 41 ○ 42 ○ 43

d. square pillar

1d ○ 38 ○ 39 ○ 40
○ 41 ○ 42 ○ 43

e. pylon

1e ○ 38 ○ 39 ○ 40
○ 41 ○ 42 ○ 43

f. screen

1f ○ 38 ○ 39 ○ 40
○ 41 ○ 42 ○ 43

PAGE
TOTAL [ ]

2. From the rough floor plans shown below, select the one that most closely matches the simple sets shown on the facing page, and fill in the corresponding bubbles. *(Note that there are floor plans that do not match any of the set photos.)*

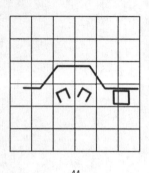

44

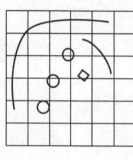

45

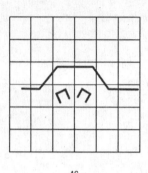

46

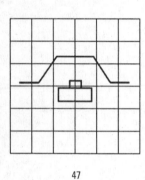

47

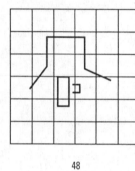

48

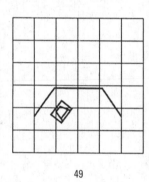

49

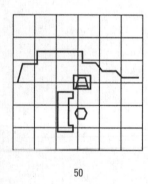

50

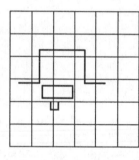

51

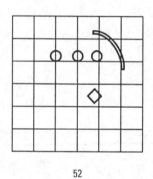

52

Course No. _____ Date _____ Name _____

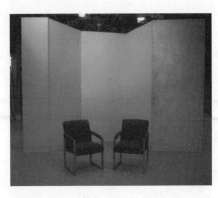

a.

b.

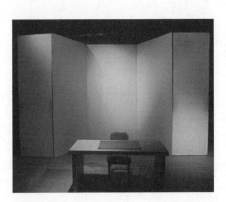

c.

d.

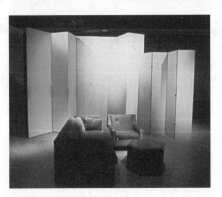

e.

f.

2a ◯ ◯ ◯ ◯ ◯
44 45 46 47 48
◯ ◯ ◯ ◯
49 50 51 52

2b ◯ ◯ ◯ ◯ ◯
44 45 46 47 48
◯ ◯ ◯ ◯
49 50 51 52

2c ◯ ◯ ◯ ◯ ◯
44 45 46 47 48
◯ ◯ ◯ ◯
49 50 51 52

2d ◯ ◯ ◯ ◯ ◯
44 45 46 47 48
◯ ◯ ◯ ◯
49 50 51 52

2e ◯ ◯ ◯ ◯ ◯
44 45 46 47 48
◯ ◯ ◯ ◯
49 50 51 52

2f ◯ ◯ ◯ ◯ ◯
44 45 46 47 48
◯ ◯ ◯ ◯
49 50 51 52

PAGE TOTAL [   ]

Select the correct answers and fill in the bubbles with the corresponding numbers.

3. To elevate scenery, properties, or action areas, we use (53) *periaktoi*
(54) *platforms* (55) *pylons.*

3 ○ ○ ○
53 54 55

4. A bookcase, the books in it, and the chair next to it are all part of (56) *set decoration* (57) *set furniture* (58) *properties.*

4 ○ ○ ○
56 57 58

5. The continuous piece of canvas or muslin stretched along two, three, or even all four studio walls to form a uniform background is referred to as (59) *a drop* (60) *canvas backing* (61) *a cyclorama.*

5 ○ ○ ○
59 60 61

6. The standard backgrounds used to simulate interior and exterior walls are called (62) *cycs* (63) *flats* (64) *drops.*

6 ○ ○ ○
62 63 64

7. Scenic pieces that can be used in a variety of configurations are called (65) *set modules* (66) *hardwall flats* (67) *set dressings.*

7 ○ ○ ○
65 66 67

8. The painting at the back of an interview set is a (68) *set prop* (69) *hand prop* (70) *set dressing.*

8 ○ ○ ○
68 69 70

9. A ground row is usually built into the (71) *control room* (72) *hardwall cyc* (73) *prop area.*

9 ○ ○ ○
71 72 73

10. The desk for the news anchor is considered a (74) *set prop* (75) *hand prop* (76) *set dressing.*

10 ○ ○ ○
74 75 76

11. The usual height for standard set units is (77) *7 feet* (78) *10 feet* (79) *14 feet.* For low-ceiling studios, it is (80) *8 feet* (81) *6 feet* (82) *12 feet. **(Fill in two bubbles.)***

11 ○ ○ ○
77 78 79
○ ○ ○
80 81 82

PAGE
TOTAL

SECTION
TOTAL

144

REVIEW QUIZ

Mark the following statements as true or false by filling in the bubbles in the
T *(for true) or* ***F*** *(for false) column.*

		T	F
1.	In many video productions, props and set dressings are more important than the background flats for indicating a certain style.	1 ○ 83	○ 84
2.	Most professional production sets, such as a news set, are constructed with hardwall flats.	2 ○ 85	○ 86
3.	A monitor is identical to a television set except that it has a sharper picture.	3 ○ 87	○ 88
4.	All active furniture should be placed at least 6 to 8 feet from the background scenery.	4 ○ 89	○ 90
5.	A well-functioning S.A. system makes a P.L. unnecessary.	5 ○ 91	○ 92
6.	Wagons can be used as platforms.	6 ○ 93	○ 94
7.	The control room must be equipped with speakers that carry the line-out audio signal.	7 ○ 95	○ 96
8.	The program objective has a great influence on the set design.	8 ○ 97	○ 98
9.	In a scenic context, jacks are electrical outlets for prop lamps.	9 ○ 99	○ 100
10.	The sound control (console) must be located as close to the director as possible.	10 ○ 101	○ 102
11.	An accurate control room clock makes the use of a stopwatch unnecessary.	11 ○ 103	○ 104
12.	A small studio does not need a smooth floor because zoom lenses make dollying unnecessary.	12 ○ 105	○ 106
13.	The switcher must be located right next to the producer's position.	13 ○ 107	○ 108
14.	The preview (or preset) and line monitors should be side-by-side in the control room.	14 ○ 109	○ 110
15.	Lashlines work well for softwall scenery but are not used for hardwall scenery.	15 ○ 111	○ 112

SECTION TOTAL [　　]

PROBLEM-SOLVING APPLICATIONS

1. You are asked by the new art professor about the feasibility of converting a classroom into a small video production studio. The classroom has no windows, normal doors, a 10-foot ceiling with standard fluorescent lighting, and a wood floor. What would you tell the professor? Be specific.

2. You are asked by the company president why you need so many monitors in the control room. She tells you that she had consulted an electronics engineer, who told her that there are switching devices that let you preview multiple video sources on a single monitor. She quotes the engineer as saying that all you really need are two monitors. How, if at all, would you defend a multimonitor stack in the control room?

3. You are to evaluate the preliminary design for a new control room (see illustration below). What, if any, changes would you recommend? Why?

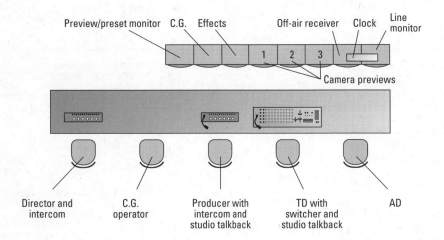

Preview/preset monitor C.G. Effects Off-air receiver Clock Line monitor

1 2 3

Camera previews

Director and intercom   C.G. operator   Producer with intercom and studio talkback   TD with switcher and studio talkback   AD

4. Using one of the forms at the back of this workbook, draw a floor plan for a weekly interview show dealing with the art and media scene in your city. The host will interview guests from theater, the music scene, radio, and television. Include a detailed prop list.

5. Draw a floor plan for a morning news set. The news anchors consist of a woman and a man, and the news content is geared more toward local gossip than international politics.

15 Production Environment: Field and Computer-generated

REVIEW OF KEY TERMS

Match each term with its appropriate definition by filling in the corresponding bubble.

1. **big remote**
2. **field production**
3. **uplink truck**
4. **remote truck**

5. **ENG**
6. **EFP**
7. **remote survey**
8. **contact person**

9. **synthetic environment**
10. **virtual reality**

A. Electronically generated settings, either through chroma key or computer.

A ○ ○ ○ ○ ○
   1 2 3 4 5
   ○ ○ ○ ○ ○
   6 7 8 9 10

B. A production of a large, scheduled event done for live transmission or live-on-tape recording.

B ○ ○ ○ ○ ○
   1 2 3 4 5
   ○ ○ ○ ○ ○
   6 7 8 9 10

C. A person who is familiar with and who can facilitate access to the remote location and the key people.

C ○ ○ ○ ○ ○
   1 2 3 4 5
   ○ ○ ○ ○ ○
   6 7 8 9 10

D. Any video production that happens outside the studio.

D ○ ○ ○ ○ ○
   1 2 3 4 5
   ○ ○ ○ ○ ○
   6 7 8 9 10

E. Computer-simulated environment with which the user can interact.

E ○ ○ ○ ○ ○
   1 2 3 4 5
   ○ ○ ○ ○ ○
   6 7 8 9 10

PAGE
TOTAL [ ]

© 2007 Thomson Wadsworth

 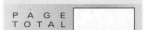

1. big remote	5. ENG	9. synthetic environment
2. field production	6. EFP	10. virtual reality
3. uplink truck	7. remote survey	
4. remote truck	8. contact person	

F. An inspection of the remote location by key production and engineering persons so that they can plan for the setup and use of production equipment.

F ○ ○ ○ ○ ○
   1 2 3 4 5
   ○ ○ ○ ○ ○
   6 7 8 9 10

G. Small vehicle that sends video and audio signals to a satellite.

G ○ ○ ○ ○ ○
   1 2 3 4 5
   ○ ○ ○ ○ ○
   6 7 8 9 10

H. The use of portable camcorders, lights, and sound equipment for the production of unplanned daily news events. Usually done for live transmission or immediate postproduction.

H ○ ○ ○ ○ ○
   1 2 3 4 5
   ○ ○ ○ ○ ○
   6 7 8 9 10

I. Video production done outside the studio that is usually shot for postproduction (not live).

I ○ ○ ○ ○ ○
   1 2 3 4 5
   ○ ○ ○ ○ ○
   6 7 8 9 10

J. The vehicle that carries the control room, audio control, VTR section, video control section, and transmission equipment.

J ○ ○ ○ ○ ○
   1 2 3 4 5
   ○ ○ ○ ○ ○
   6 7 8 9 10

PAGE TOTAL ☐

SECTION TOTAL ☐

■ REVIEW OF ENG AND EFP

Select the correct answers and fill in the bubbles with the corresponding numbers.

1. When videotaping an outside interview, your major audio concern is
   (11) *wind* (12) *ambient sounds* (13) *traffic noise.*

   1 ○ ○ ○
      11   12   13

2. Whenever possible you should white-balance your camcorder (14) *every
   time you enter a new lighting environment* (15) *before going out for a shoot*
   (16) *only when it gets dark.*

   2 ○ ○ ○
      14   15   16

3. The field production least likely to use signal transmission equipment is
   (17) *ENG* (18) *EFP* (19) *big remotes.*

   3 ○ ○ ○
      17   18   19

4. One of the important preproduction activities for EFP is (20) *striping all
   source tapes with time code* (21) *blacking all source tapes* (22) *conducting a
   remote survey.*

   4 ○ ○ ○
      20   21   22

5. In EFP the best way to light indoor activities is to (23) *use a few high-
   powered spotlights* (24) *use several low-powered floodlights* (25) *place the
   action in front of a window.*

   5 ○ ○ ○
      23   24   25

6. When the reporter uses an external hand or lavaliere mic, you (26) *should*
   (27) *should not* open the camera mic simultaneously.

   6 ○ ○
      26   27

7. A functioning P.L. intercom system is essential for (28) *ENG* (29) *EFP*
   (30) *big remotes.*

   7 ○ ○ ○
      28   29   30

8. The one field production that functions most of the time without a remote
   survey is (31) *ENG* (32) *EFP* (33) *big remotes.*

   8 ○ ○ ○
      31   32   33

9. When using a computer-generated background for live action, you must
   watch that the (34) *motion vectors* (35) *attached and cast shadows*
   (36) *colors* match between foreground and background.

   9 ○ ○ ○
      34   35   36

10. When covering a story with a field reporter, you should whenever possible
    place the reporter (37) *in a sunlit area* (38) *in front of a brightly lit background*
    (39) *in the shade.*

    10 ○ ○ ○
        37   38   39

PAGE
TOTAL [   ]

© 2007 Thomson Wadsworth

11. Analyze the following survey location sketch and select the major production hazards from the list below. Fill in the bubbles with the corresponding numbers. *(Multiple answers are possible.)*

(40) *little room for cross shooting*

(41) *plants interfering with good composition*

(42) *window causing lighting problems*

(43) *no room for VTRs*

(44) *matching color temperatures, if 3,200K fill lights are used*

(45) *computer interfering with video signal*

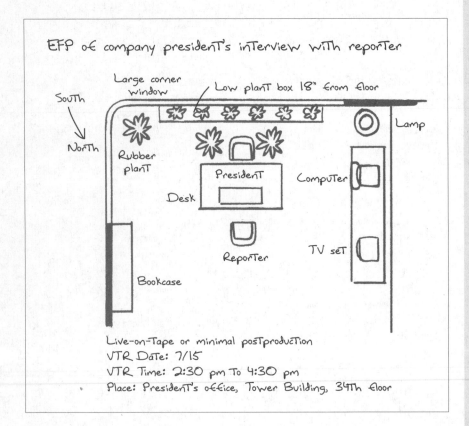

EFP of company president's interview with reporter

Large corner window — Low plant box 18" from floor

South

North

Rubber plant

President

Desk

Reporter

Computer

Lamp

TV set

Bookcase

Live-on-Tape or minimal postproduction
VTR Date: 7/15
VTR Time: 2:30 pm to 4:30 pm
Place: President's office, Tower Building, 34th floor

*Evaluate the equipment checklists for the three electronic field productions described below. Identify the **wrong equipment** or **items not needed** to take on location and fill in the bubbles with the corresponding numbers. (Multiple answers are possible.)*

12. Taping of a brief dance number to recorded music in front of city hall.

12 ○ ○ ○ ○ ○
　46　47　48　49　50
○ ○ ○ ○
51　52　53　54

CHECKLIST

(46) *3 ENG/EFP cameras*　　　　(51) *large audio console*

(47) *6 shotgun mics*　　　　　　(52) *P.A. audiotape playback system*

(48) *ESS*　　　　　　　　　　　(53) *fishpoles for mics*

(49) *3 VTRs*　　　　　　　　　　(54) *C.G.*

(50) *3 RCUs and connecting cables*

13. Live stand-up traffic report from downtown during early-afternoon rush hour.

13 ○ ○ ○ ○ ○
　55　56　57　58　59
○ ○ ○ ○
60　61　62　63

CHECKLIST

(55) *digital camcorder*　　　　　(60) *audiotape recorder*

(56) *2 VTRs*　　　　　　　　　　(61) *microwave transmission equipment*

(57) *camera mic*　　　　　　　　(62) *I.F.B. intercom*

(58) *hand mic*　　　　　　　　　(63) *C.G.*

(59) *3 portable lighting kits*

14. Taped interview of a media scholar in his hotel room for news item.

14 ○ ○ ○ ○ ○
　64　65　66　67　68
○ ○ ○ ○
69　70　71　72

CHECKLIST

(64) *digital camcorder*　　　　　(69) *portable audio mixer*

(65) *VTR*　　　　　　　　　　　(70) *videotape or other recording media*

(66) *portable lighting kit*　　　　(71) *batteries*

(67) *RCU*　　　　　　　　　　　(72) *two preview monitors*

(68) *lavaliere mic*

PAGE TOTAL ▢

SECTION TOTAL ▢

Mark the following statements as true or false by filling in the bubbles in the
T *(for true) or **F** (for false) column.*

	T	F

1. Because in EFP the director can check the camera viewfinder, a playback monitor is not necessary.

   1 ○ 73 ○ 74

2. Remote surveys are especially important for ENG.

   2 ○ 75 ○ 76

3. If possible, you should do the survey for an outdoor remote during the time the actual production will take place.

   3 ○ 77 ○ 78

4. A satellite uplink truck is essential for transmitting a live ENG pickup from a remote location.

   4 ○ 79 ○ 80

5. Contrary to ENG, EFP does not require keeping accurate field logs.

   5 ○ 81 ○ 82

6. ENG and EFP require the same level of preproduction.

   6 ○ 83 ○ 84

7. An I.F.B. intercom system is essential for successful EFP.

   7 ○ 85 ○ 86

8. A remote truck is usually powered by an external power source.

   8 ○ 87 ○ 88

9. A well-equipped remote truck must contain a compact program control center.

   9 ○ 89 ○ 90

10. All synthetic environments must originally be lens-generated.

   10 ○ 91 ○ 92

11. A remote survey is important for the technical crew but not the nontechnical people.

   11 ○ 93 ○ 94

12. Keeping an accurate field log is especially important for a live remote pickup.

   12 ○ 95 ○ 96

13. A contact person is necessary for EFP and big remotes.

   13 ○ 97 ○ 98

14. The position of the sun is an important factor in surveys for outdoor remotes.

   14 ○ 99 ○ 100

15. There is no difference between a lens-generated and a computer-generated environment.

   15 ○ 101 ○ 102

SECTION TOTAL [ ]

PROBLEM-SOLVING APPLICATIONS

1. To get a good overhead shot of a parade, you would like to place one of the cameras in the twentieth-floor window of a nearby hotel. The TD informs you that the hotel manager has nothing against your renting the room for the day and setting up the camera, but he will not allow any cable runs either inside or outside the hotel. What would you suggest?

2. To be "on the cutting edge" with his employees, the new company president would like to speak to them from a fantasy landscape yet remain behind his familiar desk. Can you oblige the president's request? If so, how? If not, why not?

3. You are asked to help draw up specifications for a new remote truck for a college broadcasting department that specializes in telecasting all kinds of college sports. What questions should you ask before making a recommendation? Why?

4. The new PA is very upset about your failure to request an adequate P.L. system for the single-camera EFP in the university student union. What would you tell the PA? Why?

5. Conduct a detailed remote survey of two of the following events: a local school board meeting; a rock concert in a city park; a modern dance performance in front of city hall; an interview with a university president in his or her office; the gala opening of a new computer store; a wedding in a local church; a basketball game in a high-school or college gym.

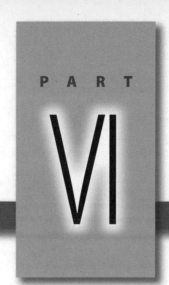

Production Control: Talent and Directing

16 Talent, Clothing, and Makeup

REVIEW OF KEY TERMS

Match each term with its appropriate definition by filling in the corresponding bubble.

1. I.F.B.
2. moiré effect
3. actor

4. performer
5. talent
6. teleprompter

7. blocking
8. foundation
9. cue card

A. A person who appears on-camera in dramatic roles.

A ○ ○ ○ ○ ○
   1 2 3 4 5
   ○ ○ ○ ○
   6 7 8 9

B. Color vibrations that occur when narrow, contrasting stripes of a design interfere with the frequency of the scanning lines of the video system.

B ○ ○ ○ ○ ○
   1 2 3 4 5
   ○ ○ ○ ○
   6 7 8 9

C. A person who appears on-camera in nondramatic shows.

C ○ ○ ○ ○ ○
   1 2 3 4 5
   ○ ○ ○ ○
   6 7 8 9

D. A large hand-lettered card that contains copy, usually held next to the camera lens by floor personnel.

D ○ ○ ○ ○ ○
   1 2 3 4 5
   ○ ○ ○ ○
   6 7 8 9

E. A makeup base, normally done with water-soluble pancake makeup.

E ○ ○ ○ ○ ○
   1 2 3 4 5
   ○ ○ ○ ○
   6 7 8 9

PAGE
TOTAL [ ]

© 2007 Thomson Wadsworth

1. I.F.B.	4. performer	7. blocking
2. moiré effect	5. talent	8. foundation
3. actor	6. teleprompter	9. cue card

F. A prompting system that allows communication with talent while on the air.

F   ① ② ③ ④ ⑤   ⑥ ⑦ ⑧ ⑨

G. A device that projects the moving copy over the camera lens so that the talent can read it without losing eye contact with the viewer.

G   ① ② ③ ④ ⑤   ⑥ ⑦ ⑧ ⑨

H. Carefully worked-out movement and actions of the talent and all mobile video equipment used in a scene.

H   ① ② ③ ④ ⑤   ⑥ ⑦ ⑧ ⑨

I. Collective name for all performers and actors who appear regularly on television.

I   ① ② ③ ④ ⑤   ⑥ ⑦ ⑧ ⑨

PAGE TOTAL

SECTION TOTAL

REVIEW OF PERFORMANCE TECHNIQUES

1. The following figures show various cues as given to the talent by the floor manager. From the list below, select the specific cue illustrated and fill in the bubble with the corresponding number.

(10) *standby*   (15) *wind up*

(11) *cue*   (16) *cut*

(12) *on time*   (17) *5 minutes left*

(13) *speed up*   (18) *30 seconds left*

(14) *stretch*   (19) *15 seconds left*

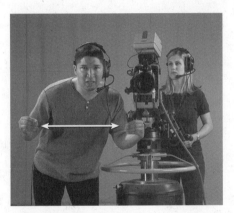

a. Pulls hands apart

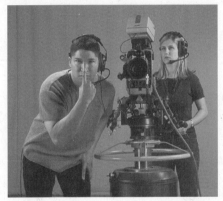

b.

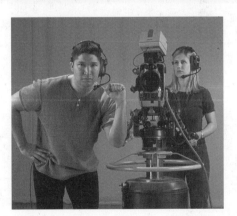

c.

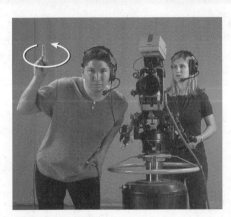

d. Rotates hand

1a ○ ○ ○ ○ ○
    10 11 12 13 14
    ○ ○ ○ ○ ○
    15 16 17 18 19

1b ○ ○ ○ ○ ○
    10 11 12 13 14
    ○ ○ ○ ○ ○
    15 16 17 18 19

1c ○ ○ ○ ○ ○
    10 11 12 13 14
    ○ ○ ○ ○ ○
    15 16 17 18 19

1d ○ ○ ○ ○ ○
    10 11 12 13 14
    ○ ○ ○ ○ ○
    15 16 17 18 19

P A G E
T O T A L

(10) *standby*
(11) *cue*
(12) *on time*
(13) *speed up*
(14) *stretch*

(15) *wind up*
(16) *cut*
(17) *5 minutes left*
(18) *30 seconds left*
(19) *15 seconds left*

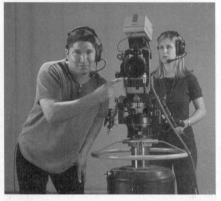

e.

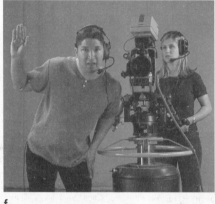

f.

1e ○ ○ ○ ○ ○
　 10 11 12 13 14
　 ○ ○ ○ ○ ○
　 15 16 17 18 19

1f ○ ○ ○ ○ ○
　 10 11 12 13 14
　 ○ ○ ○ ○ ○
　 15 16 17 18 19

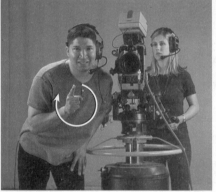

g. Rotates hand with extended
index finger

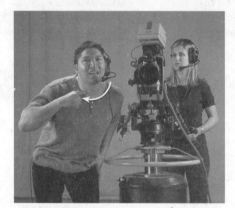

h. Pulls index finger across throat

1g ○ ○ ○ ○ ○
　 10 11 12 13 14
　 ○ ○ ○ ○ ○
　 15 16 17 18 19

1h ○ ○ ○ ○ ○
　 10 11 12 13 14
　 ○ ○ ○ ○ ○
　 15 16 17 18 19

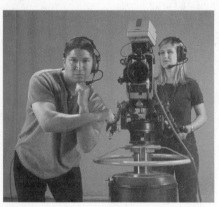

i.

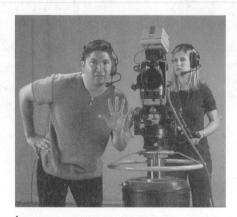

j.

1i ○ ○ ○ ○ ○
　 10 11 12 13 14
　 ○ ○ ○ ○ ○
　 15 16 17 18 19

1j ○ ○ ○ ○ ○
　 10 11 12 13 14
　 ○ ○ ○ ○ ○
　 15 16 17 18 19

PAGE
TOTAL

2. The following figures show various cues as given to the talent by the floor manager. From the list below, select the specific cue illustrated and fill in the bubble with the corresponding number.

(20) *VTR rolling*

(21) *closer*

(22) *back*

(23) *walk*

(24) *stop*

(25) *OK*

(26) *speak up*

(27) *tone down*

(28) *closer to mic*

(29) *keep talking*

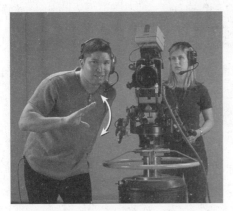

a. Fingers open and close like a bird beak

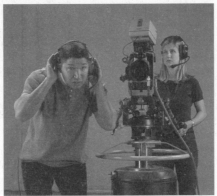

b.

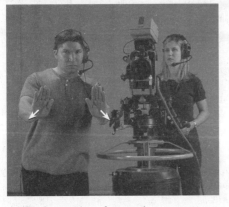

c. Pushes palms forward

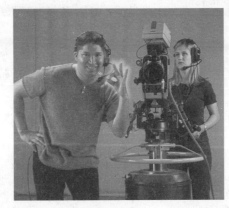

d.

2a ◯ ◯ ◯ ◯ ◯
   20 21 22 23 24
◯ ◯ ◯ ◯ ◯
25 26 27 28 29

2b ◯ ◯ ◯ ◯ ◯
   20 21 22 23 24
◯ ◯ ◯ ◯ ◯
25 26 27 28 29

2c ◯ ◯ ◯ ◯ ◯
   20 21 22 23 24
◯ ◯ ◯ ◯ ◯
25 26 27 28 29

2d ◯ ◯ ◯ ◯ ◯
   20 21 22 23 24
◯ ◯ ◯ ◯ ◯
25 26 27 28 29

PAGE TOTAL [ ]

(20) *VTR rolling*		(25) *OK*			
(21) *closer*		(26) *speak up*			
(22) *back*		(27) *tone down*			
(23) *walk*		(28) *closer to mic*			
(24) *stop*		(29) *keep talking*			

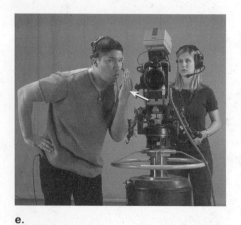

e.

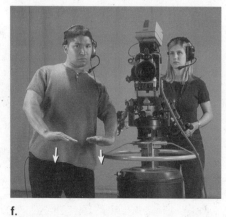

f.

2e
20 21 22 23 24
25 26 27 28 29

2f
20 21 22 23 24
25 26 27 28 29

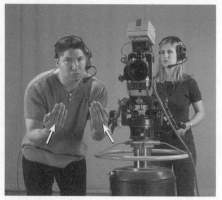

g. Pulls hands toward body

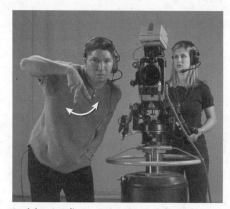

h. Moves fingers back and forth

2g
20 21 22 23 24
25 26 27 28 29

2h
20 21 22 23 24
25 26 27 28 29

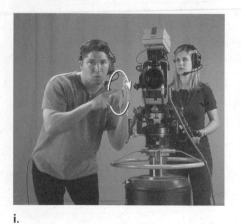

i.

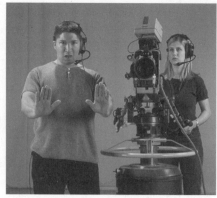

j.

2i
20 21 22 23 24
25 26 27 28 29

2j
20 21 22 23 24
25 26 27 28 29

PAGE
TOTAL

Select the correct answers and fill in the bubbles with the corresponding numbers.

3. When wearing a lavaliere mic, you should (30) *maintain your audio level regardless of how far the camera is away from you* (31) *increase your volume when the camera gets farther away from you* (32) *speak more softly when the camera is relatively close to you.*

3 ◯ ◯ ◯
   30   31   32

4. When asked for an audio level, you should (33) *blow into the mic* (34) *count quickly to five* (35) *recite your opening remarks at on-air levels.*

4 ◯ ◯ ◯
   33   34   35

5. When you receive cues during the actual videotaping that are different from the rehearsed ones, you should (36) *execute the action as rehearsed* (37) *promptly follow the floor manager's cues* (38) *check with the director.*

5 ◯ ◯ ◯
   36   37   38

6. From the list below, select the microphone most appropriate for the various performance and acting tasks and fill in the bubbles with the corresponding numbers.

(39) *desk mics*   (42) *stand mic*

(40) *hand mic*   (43) *lavaliere mic*

(41) *fishpole mic*

a. Interview with a celebrity at a busy airport gate.

6a ◯ ◯ ◯ ◯ ◯
    39 40 41 42 43

b. News anchor who remains seated throughout newscast.

6b ◯ ◯ ◯ ◯ ◯
    39 40 41 42 43

c. Moderating a panel discussion with six guests.

6c ◯ ◯ ◯ ◯ ◯
    39 40 41 42 43

d. Lead guitarist of a rock band who also sings and talks to the audience.

6d ◯ ◯ ◯ ◯ ◯
    39 40 41 42 43

e. Two actors doing a brief outdoor scene.

6e ◯ ◯ ◯ ◯ ◯
    39 40 41 42 43

7. If you do not use I.F.B. during a studio production, you should take your opening cues from (44) *the camera operator* (45) *the floor manager* (46) *the tally lights.*

7 ◯ ◯ ◯
   44   45   46

8. For the talent the most accurate indicator of the camera's field of view is (47) *the relative distance between talent and camera* (48) *the floor manager's cues* (49) *the studio monitor.*

8 ◯ ◯ ◯
   47   48   49

9. When demonstrating a small object, you should (50) *hold it as close to the lens as possible* (51) *keep it as steady as possible or on the display table* (52) *move it slowly toward the camera.*

9 ◯ ◯ ◯
   50   51   52

PAGE TOTAL [ ]

SECTION TOTAL [ ]

Chapter 16 — *Talent, Clothing, and Makeup*

10. Read the following copy into a mirror or, better, into a television camera with a teleprompter, at least three times. Video-record your performances. Time your narration with a stopwatch and try to match your times with the ones given in subsequent readings.

a. news copy

Package: Australia Earth Mover

<u>VIDEO</u>   <u>AUDIO</u>

TALENT O/C   IN SOUTHERN AUSTRALIA,
(ON CAMERA)   ENGINEERS ARE RAVING ABOUT A NEW
                        DEVELOPMENT...A GIANT EARTH MOVER
                        THAT HAS NO WHEELS. CHIEF ENGINEER
                        FRED STEINER SAYS HE OBSERVED HOW A
                        CENTIPEDE TRAVELS AND SIMPLY COPIED
                        ITS MOVEMENTS.

SERVER FILE
0120
VO   THE MANY LEGS ENABLE THE MACHINE TO
                        NEGOTIATE DITCHES, BUSHES, AND EVEN
                        GOOD-SIZED BOULDERS WITHOUT SPILLING
                        ITS LOAD OR TIPPING OVER.

                        JOHN HEWITT TALKED TO THE DRIVER...OR
                        RIDER?...OF THE MONSTER CENTIPEDE...
SERVER FILE
0121
SOS
(SOUND ON SOURCE)
1:45

Given time: 29 seconds

Your first reading: _____ seconds

Your second reading: _____ seconds

Your third reading: _____ seconds

b. introduction to a weekly sports show

```
VIDEO              AUDIO


STANDARD
OPENING
SERVER FILE
SP 772


WALTER O/C         Hi, I'm Alex Walter. Welcome
                   to Sports at Four. Today we have
                   with us the world's most prominent
                   and amazing


CU MESSNER         mountain climber--Reinhold Messner.
                   He will talk to us about how he
                   prepared for his extreme climbs and
C.G.: EVEREST      what he thought and felt when he
                   climbed--often alone--the big walls of
                   the world's highest peaks.


WALTER O/C         He has brought with him some of the
                   best mountain-climbing footage I have
                   ever seen--and he will share it with
                   us. We will also see where Reinhold
                   lives and what he does now. All coming
                   up next on Sports at Four.


-----------------------------------------------------------
SERVER FILE        COMMERCIAL #1
SP 844
-----------------------------------------------------------
```

Given time: 35 seconds

Your first reading: _____ seconds

Your second reading: _____ seconds

Your third reading: _____ seconds

c. commercial
(Note that this commercial represents a high-pressure pitch and requires fast reading.)

VIDEO	AUDIO
CHROMA KEY ESS 64: CARS	
CU OF BAKER ZOOM OUT TO MS	Hi, I'm Tom Baker of Baker Dodge to talk to you about automobile leasing. It can mean lower monthly payments, and it lets you keep that down payment for other things you need.
CUT TO C.G.: LOWER MONTHLY PAYMENTS	
CUT TO ESS 65: CAR 1 ESS 66: CAR 2	For example, you can lease this brand-new beauty for only 300 dollars per month or this air-conditioned luxury car for only 499 dollars per month--and we'll even buy your old car and give you the cash!
CUT TO CU OF BAKER + CHROMA KEY ESS 64	So come on down and drive away your dream car.
CUT TO C.G. SIGNATURE	It's only at Baker Dodge in Dodge City. Come right now and save!

Given time: 30 seconds

Your first reading: _____ seconds

Your second reading: _____ seconds

Your third reading: _____ seconds

REVIEW OF PERFORMANCE AND ACTING TECHNIQUES

Select the correct answers and fill in the bubbles with the corresponding numbers.

1. When doing an O/S or cross-shooting scene, you must adjust your blocking so that you see (53) *the key light* (54) *the floor manager* (55) *the camera lens.*

1 ○ 53 ○ 54 ○ 55

2. When substituting for the regular host of a studio talk show for the first time, you should (56) *discuss the lighting with the LD* (57) *verify the specific cues with the floor manager* (58) *test the quality of the microphone used.*

2 ○ 56 ○ 57 ○ 58

3. When you receive the floor manager's time cue, you should (59) *give the floor manager a brief nod to acknowledge the cue* (60) *verify it by glancing at the clock* (61) *do nothing but adjust your performance to the remaining time.*

3 ○ 59 ○ 60 ○ 61

4. When you can't see the teleprompter well enough, you should (62) *have the camera move closer to you* (63) *ask the operator to slow down the scroll* (64) *have the font made bigger.*

4 ○ 62 ○ 63 ○ 64

5. To keep eye contact with the viewer when cameras are switched on you, you need to (65) *follow the tally lights* (66) *follow the floor manager's cues* (67) *listen to the producer's I.F.B. cues.*

5 ○ 65 ○ 66 ○ 67

6. To establish eye contact with the viewer, you need to pretend to (68) *look through the lens* (69) *converse with the floor manager* (70) *converse with the camera operator.*

6 ○ 68 ○ 69 ○ 70

7. Pretend that you (person A) are receiving a telephone call from person B. In this scene we see and hear only A (you) but not B. Using exactly the same dialogue (see the script on the following page), adapt your delivery and acting style to at least two of the following circumstances:

a. B calls to tell you that she had her first novel published.

b. B has quit her job.

c. B has just wrecked your new car.

d. B has called off the wedding.

e. B has won big in the lottery.

f. B has been arrested.

g. B has lost her job.

h. B has won an Emmy for innovative productions.

Place the scene anywhere you like. You may do well to write the other part of the phone conversation so that you can listen and respond more convincingly.

SECTION TOTAL ☐

© 2007 Thomson Wadsworth

PHONE CONVERSATION

Hello?
Hi.
Fine, and you?
Good.
No.
No, really. It's always a good time when you call.
I beg your pardon?
You must be kidding.
Yes.
No.
What does Chris say to all this?
No. Should I?
I don't know.
Perhaps.
You want me to come over now?
Yes. Really.
Well, this changes things somewhat.
I think so.
I'm not so sure.
Yes. No. I...
All right. But not...
OK.
If you think this is...
Definitely.
Good-bye...When?
No. Really.
Good-bye.

REVIEW OF CLOTHING AND MAKEUP

Select the correct answers and fill in the bubbles with the corresponding numbers.

1. When doing makeup, you should have lighting conditions that are the same as or close to those of (71) *your customary makeup room* (72) *the actual production environment* (73) *normal 3,200K studio lights.*

1 ○ ○ ○
   71 72 73

2. During a green-backdrop chroma key, you should not wear (74) *red* (75) *blue* (76) *green* because this color will let the background show through during the key.

2 ○ ○ ○
   74 75 76

3. The dress of a pop singer has many rhinestones that sparkle under the colored stage lights. This dress is (77) *acceptable* (78) *unacceptable* because (79) *the digital camera can handle small areas of extreme bright light* (80) *there is too much brightness contrast* (81) *it will result in moiré patterns* (82) *it will reinforce the stage lighting.* **(Fill in two bubbles.)**

3 ○ ○
   77 78
  ○ ○ ○ ○
  79 80 81 82

4. One of the most widely used makeup foundations is (83) *pancake* (84) *grease base* (85) *oil-based foundation.*

4 ○ ○ ○
   83 84 85

5. Clothing with thin, highly contrasting stripes or checkered patterns is (86) *acceptable* (87) *not acceptable* because (88) *the CCD camera can handle such a contrast quite easily* (89) *it provides exciting patterns* (90) *it results in moiré color vibrations* (91) *it is too detailed for the camera to see.* **(Fill in two bubbles.)**

5 ○ ○
   86 87
  ○ ○ ○ ○
  88 89 90 91

SECTION TOTAL [ ]

Mark the following statements as true or false by filling in the bubbles in the
T (for true) or **F** (for false) column.

	T	F
1	○ 92	○ 93

1. In a cross shot, you should stand on your mark even if you can't see the
camera lens.

| **2** | ○ 94 | ○ 95 |

2. You can ignore the time cues by the floor manager so long as you can see the
studio clock.

| **3** | ○ 96 | ○ 97 |

3. A close-up speeds up all movements.

| **4** | ○ 98 | ○ 99 |

4. Because you never know what you will be asked to read in an audition, you
should not prepare for it but can and should rely on the energy of the moment
during the audition.

| **5** | ○ 100 | ○ 101 |

5. When working with a teleprompter, it is best to move the camera as close as
possible to the talent.

| **6** | ○ 102 | ○ 103 |

6. When on a close-up, you need to keep your actions tighter and slower
than normal.

| **7** | ○ 104 | ○ 105 |

7. What you wear is really unimportant when simply auditioning for a role.

| **8** | ○ 106 | ○ 107 |

8. Because of possible moiré effects, you should avoid wearing high-contrast
striped patterns on-camera.

| **9** | ○ 108 | ○ 109 |

9. A "cut" cue from the floor manager means that the director is cutting
(switching) to the next camera.

| **10** | ○ 110 | ○ 111 |

10. If you discover that you are talking to the wrong camera, you should look
down and then look up into the on-the-air camera.

| **11** | ○ 112 | ○ 113 |

11. You should try to get the floor manager's attention when you think that you
should have received a time cue.

| **12** | ○ 114 | ○ 115 |

12. The best way to give an audio level is to quickly count to five.

| **13** | ○ 116 | ○ 117 |

13. *Talent* refers to both actors and performers.

| **14** | ○ 118 | ○ 119 |

14. In contrast to television performers, actors always portray someone else.

**SECTION
TOTAL** [ ]

PROBLEM-SOLVING APPLICATIONS

1. The talent for the new weekly Opera Review show arrives in a bright red dress. She will interview the star tenor in the dimly lit backstage area of the opera house. Although the camera operator is using a small three-chip digital camcorder, he is somewhat concerned about the talent's attire. Why? What would you suggest?

2. The ENG camera operator is concerned about proper fill light for you, the reporter, during a live transmission of a traffic report on the fog-shrouded Golden Gate Bridge, so he asks for an additional person to handle the fill light. Do you share the camera operator's concern? If so, why? If not, why not?

3. The ENG camera operator suggests that you do your stand-up report right in front of the bright, sunlit wall of city hall. According to the camera operator, the automatic-iris control would guarantee the high-key lighting effect which, in turn, would reflect the upbeat story you have to tell. Do you agree with the camera operator? If so, why? If not, why not?

4. To practice blocking, write down a series of moves that carry you around your kitchen. For example, you can start at the stove, then get the teakettle out of the cupboard, put it on the stove, go back to pick up the telephone, put down the telephone to answer the door, and so forth. Try to hit the same marks each time you go through the routine. If possible, have a friend videotape your blocking maneuvers from the same camera position. You can then compare the tapes and check how accurate your blocking was. As part of the same exercise, you can use various props (kitchen utensils) and see how the camera's field of view (LS to ECU) will influence your handling of props.

5. Do your favorite monologue and videotape it (or, better, have someone else tape it) first in a loose medium shot, then in a CU, and finally in an ECU. Analyze how the camera's field of view changes your delivery and try to adjust your acting to each circumstance. Note especially the relative speed of your delivery and your facial expressions.

17 Putting It All Together: Directing

REVIEW OF KEY TERMS

Match each term with its appropriate definition by filling in the corresponding bubble.

1. dry run
2. time line
3. visualization
4. shot sheet
5. walk-through/camera rehearsal
6. single-column script
7. two-column documentary script
8. camera rehearsal
9. blocking
10. multicamera directing
11. single-camera directing

A. A combination of orientation session and follow-up runthrough with equipment.

A ○ ○ ○ ○
   1 2 3 4
   ○ ○ ○ ○
   5 6 7 8
   ○ ○ ○
   9 10 11

B. Traditional television script format with both audio and video information.

B ○ ○ ○ ○
   1 2 3 4
   ○ ○ ○ ○
   5 6 7 8
   ○ ○ ○
   9 10 11

C. Determining the positions and the actions of talent and equipment.

C ○ ○ ○ ○
   1 2 3 4
   ○ ○ ○ ○
   5 6 7 8
   ○ ○ ○
   9 10 11

PAGE TOTAL ☐

D. Same as dress rehearsal.

D
1 2 3 4
5 6 7 8
9 10 11

E. Coordinating the simultaneous use of several cameras from the control room.

E
1 2 3 4
5 6 7 8
9 10 11

F. A list of specific framings and movements for each camera used in the production.

F
1 2 3 4
5 6 7 8
9 10 11

G. Rehearsal without equipment.

G
1 2 3 4
5 6 7 8
9 10 11

H. Traditional script format for television plays.

H
1 2 3 4
5 6 7 8
9 10 11

PAGE TOTAL

1. dry run	5. walk-through/camera rehearsal	8. camera rehearsal
2. time line		9. blocking
3. visualization	6. single-column script	10. multicamera directing
4. shot sheet	7. two-column documentary script	11. single-camera directing

I. A schedule of various production activities.

I ○ ○ ○ ○
   1 2 3 4
   ○ ○ ○ ○
   5 6 7 8
   ○ ○ ○
   9 10 11

J. The mental image of a shot.

J ○ ○ ○ ○
   1 2 3 4
   ○ ○ ○ ○
   5 6 7 8
   ○ ○ ○
   9 10 11

K. Guiding the use of a single camcorder for videotaping scripted events for postproduction.

K ○ ○ ○ ○
   1 2 3 4
   ○ ○ ○ ○
   5 6 7 8
   ○ ○ ○
   9 10 11

PAGE TOTAL ☐

SECTION TOTAL ☐

REVIEW OF VISUALIZATION, CONTEXT, AND SEQUENCING

1. The following sketches show visualizations that change with different contexts. Fill in the bubbles that most closely match each visualization with its most appropriate context.

Set 1:

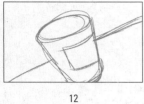
12

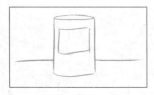
13

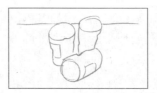
14

a. This dog food is rich in vitamins.

1a ○ 12　○ 13　○ 14

b. Danger! This might be a bomb!

1b ○ 12　○ 13　○ 14

c. This can looks old—let's throw it away.

1c ○ 12　○ 13　○ 14

Set 2:

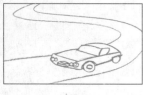
15

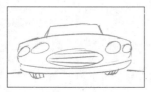
16

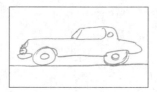
17

d. As a luxury car, it is in a class by itself.

1d ○ 15　○ 16　○ 17

e. It handles like a sports car.

1e ○ 15　○ 16　○ 17

f. It has a powerful engine.

1f ○ 15　○ 16　○ 17

SECTION TOTAL [　]

REVIEW OF INTERPRETING STORYBOARDS

1. Each of the following four storyboards shows one or several major problems. Fill in the bubbles whose numbers correspond with one or more of these major problems: (18) *poor continuity and disturbance of the mental map* (19) *wrong field-of-view designation* (20) *wrong above- or below-eye-level camera position.* (Note: Storyboards may exhibit more than one problem.)

Storyboard a Man and woman looking at each other

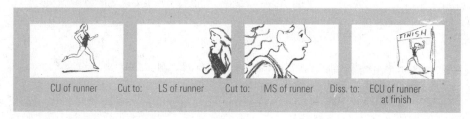

CU of woman   Cut to: CU of man   Cut to: 2-shot   Cut to: Tighter 2-shot

1a ○ 18   ○ 19   ○ 20

Storyboard b Runner finishing in first place

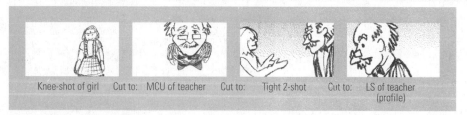

CU of runner   Cut to: LS of runner   Cut to: MS of runner   Diss. to: ECU of runner at finish

1b ○ 18   ○ 19   ○ 20

Storyboard c Teacher talking to girl

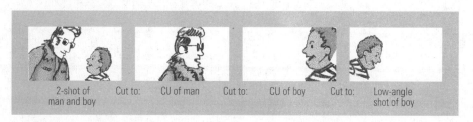

Knee-shot of girl   Cut to: MCU of teacher   Cut to: Tight 2-shot   Cut to: LS of teacher (profile)

1c ○ 18   ○ 19   ○ 20

Storyboard d Rock star talking to fan

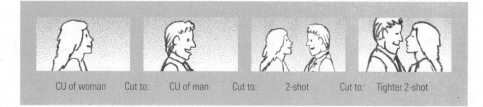

2-shot of man and boy   Cut to: CU of man   Cut to: CU of boy   Cut to: Low-angle shot of boy

1d ○ 18   ○ 19   ○ 20

SECTION TOTAL [ ]

REVIEW OF SCRIPT MARKING

1. Match each field-of-view designation with its appropriate full term by filling in the bubble with the corresponding number.

(21) cross-shot
(22) over-the-shoulder
    shot

(23) long shot
(24) extreme
    close-up

(25) medium shot
(26) extreme long shot
(27) close-up

a. CU

1a   ○ ○ ○ ○
     21 22 23 24
     ○ ○ ○
     25 26 27

b. MS

1b   ○ ○ ○ ○
     21 22 23 24
     ○ ○ ○
     25 26 27

c. O/S

1c   ○ ○ ○ ○
     21 22 23 24
     ○ ○ ○
     25 26 27

d. X/S

1d   ○ ○ ○ ○
     21 22 23 24
     ○ ○ ○
     25 26 27

e. ECU

1e   ○ ○ ○ ○
     21 22 23 24
     ○ ○ ○
     25 26 27

f. LS

1f   ○ ○ ○ ○
     21 22 23 24
     ○ ○ ○
     25 26 27

g. ELS

1g   ○ ○ ○ ○
     21 22 23 24
     ○ ○ ○
     25 26 27

PAGE
TOTAL

Select the correct answers and fill in the bubbles with the corresponding numbers.

2. The script markings in the following figure are (28) *acceptable*
(29) *unacceptable* because they (30) *are too small* (31) *have unnecessary or*
redundant cues (32) *are in the wrong place* (33) *show large, essential cues.*
(Fill in two bubbles.)

2   ◯   ◯
   28   29

   ◯   ◯   ◯   ◯
   30 31 32 33

JOHN

What's the matter?   *Ready camera 1*
                            Ready to cue Tammy

TAMMY
                         Cue Tammy and
Nothing.   *take camera 1*

JOHN

What do you mean, "nothing"? I can feel something is wrong.

TAMMY   *Ready to cue John*
               Ready to take camera 2

Well, I am glad you have some feeling left.

JOHN   *Cue John and take*
              camera 2

What's that supposed to mean?

TAMMY

Please, let's not start that again.

JOHN

Start what again?

TAMMY   *Ready to take camera 3*
                 for a two-shot

Well, I guess it's time to talk.   *Take camera 3*

JOHN

What do you think we have been doing all this time?

PAGE
TOTAL

SECTION
TOTAL

© 2007 Thomson Wadsworth

REVIEW OF DIRECTOR'S TERMINOLOGY

1. From the list below, select the director's visualization cue necessary to adjust the picture on the left screen to the picture on the right screen (in pairs from a through l) and fill in the bubbles with the corresponding numbers.

(34) tilt up   (39) zoom out   (43) pedestal up
(35) tilt down   (40) truck right   or crane up
(36) dolly in   (41) arc left   (44) pan left
(37) dolly out   (42) pedestal down or   (45) pan right
(38) zoom in   crane down

a.

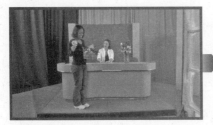 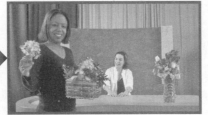

1a

○	○	○	○
34	35	36	37
○	○	○	○
38	39	40	41
○	○	○	○
42	43	44	45

b.

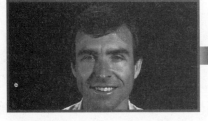 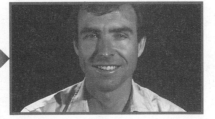

1b

○	○	○	○
34	35	36	37
○	○	○	○
38	39	40	41
○	○	○	○
42	43	44	45

c.

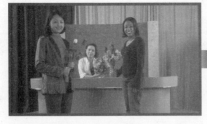 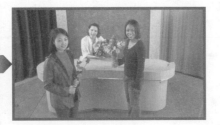

1c

○	○	○	○
34	35	36	37
○	○	○	○
38	39	40	41
○	○	○	○
42	43	44	45

P A G E
T O T A L

d.

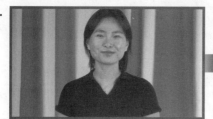 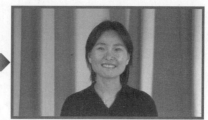

1d
○ ○ ○ ○
34 35 36 37
○ ○ ○ ○
38 39 40 41
○ ○ ○ ○
42 43 44 45

e.

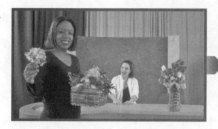 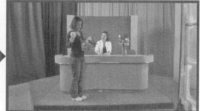

1e
○ ○ ○ ○
34 35 36 37
○ ○ ○ ○
38 39 40 41
○ ○ ○ ○
42 43 44 45

f.

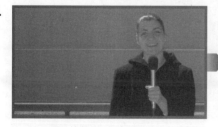 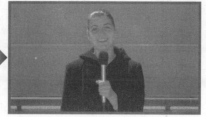

1f
○ ○ ○ ○
34 35 36 37
○ ○ ○ ○
38 39 40 41
○ ○ ○ ○
42 43 44 45

g.

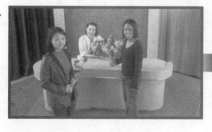 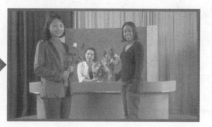

1g
○ ○ ○ ○
34 35 36 37
○ ○ ○ ○
38 39 40 41
○ ○ ○ ○
42 43 44 45

PAGE TOTAL _____

© 2007 Thomson Wadsworth

(34) tilt up	(39) zoom out	(43) pedestal up
(35) tilt down	(40) truck right	or crane up
(36) dolly in	(41) arc left	(44) pan left
(37) dolly out	(42) pedestal down	(45) pan right
(38) zoom in	or crane down	

h.
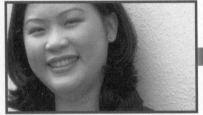 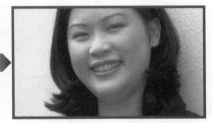

1h
○ ○ ○ ○
34 35 36 37
○ ○ ○ ○
38 39 40 41
○ ○ ○ ○
42 43 44 45

i.
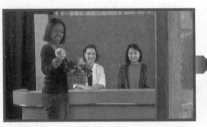 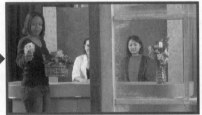

1i
○ ○ ○ ○
34 35 36 37
○ ○ ○ ○
38 39 40 41
○ ○ ○ ○
42 43 44 45

j.
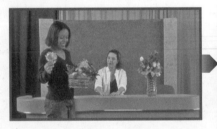 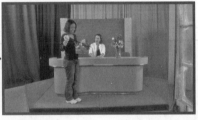

1j
○ ○ ○ ○
34 35 36 37
○ ○ ○ ○
38 39 40 41
○ ○ ○ ○
42 43 44 45

PAGE
TOTAL

(34) tilt up	(39) zoom out	(43) pedestal up
(35) tilt down	(40) truck right	or crane up
(36) dolly in	(41) arc left	(44) pan left
(37) dolly out	(42) pedestal down	(45) pan right
(38) zoom in	or crane down	

k.

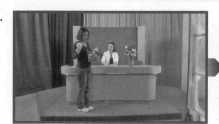 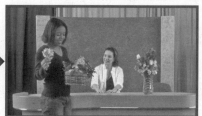

1k ◯ ◯ ◯ ◯
    34 35 36 37
    ◯ ◯ ◯ ◯
    38 39 40 41
    ◯ ◯ ◯ ◯
    42 43 44 45

l.

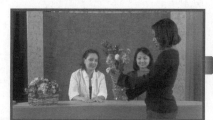 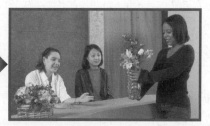

1l ◯ ◯ ◯ ◯
    34 35 36 37
    ◯ ◯ ◯ ◯
    38 39 40 41
    ◯ ◯ ◯ ◯
    42 43 44 45

PAGE
TOTAL [   ]

2. From the list below, select the correct director's cues to the floor manager by filling in the corresponding bubbles. *(The talent consists of two men and two women. Multiple answers are possible.)*

(46) Ready to cue Mary. Cue Mary.
(47) Ready to cue him. Cue him.
(48) Make him talk faster.
(49) Move her stage-right.
(50) Turn the can counterclockwise.
(51) Have two of them come closer to the camera.

2 ○ 46 ○ 47 ○ 48   ○ 49 ○ 50 ○ 51

3. From the list below, select the correct director's switching cues by filling in the corresponding bubbles. *(Multiple answers are possible.)*

(52) Ready to take camera two. Take camera two.
(53) Ready three. Take three.
(54) Ready one. Dissolve to one.
(55) Ready to go to black. Go to black.
(56) Ready wipe. Dissolve to two.
(57) Ready to change C.G. page. Change page.

3 ○ 52 ○ 53 ○ 54   ○ 55 ○ 56 ○ 57

4. From the list below, select the director who uses the correct sequence of cues for the opening of a two-camera (C1 and C2) interview and fill in the corresponding bubble. *(There is a title key for the guest. Assume that the crew has received a general standby cue and that bars and tone have already been recorded on the tape by the AD.)*

(58) *Director A:* "Ready to take C.G. Slate. Take slate. Ready black. Black. Beeper. Ready to come up on one CU of host—take one. Cue host. Ready two [on guest]. Take two. Cue guest. Key title. Take one."

(59) *Director B:* "Ready to roll VTR. Roll VTR. Ready C.G. Slate. Read slate. Ready black. Ready beeper. To black. Beeper. Ready to come up on one. Up on one. Ready two. Take two. Key. Lose key. Ready one. Take one."

(60) *Director C:* "Ready to roll VTR. Roll VTR. Ready C.G. Slate. Take C.G. Read slate. Ready black. Change page [C.G.]. Ready beeper. To black. Beeper. One, CU of host. Ready to come up on one. Open mic, cue host, up on one. Two, CU of guest. Ready two. Ready to key C.G. Take two, key. Lose key. Ready one, two-shot. Take one."

4 ○ 58 ○ 59 ○ 60

PAGE TOTAL [　　　]

SECTION TOTAL [　　　]

REVIEW OF REHEARSAL TECHNIQUES

Select the correct answers and fill in the bubbles with the corresponding numbers.

1. Blocking rehearsals are most efficiently conducted (61) *from the control room* (62) *on the studio floor or in a rehearsal hall* (63) *on the actual studio set.*

   1 ○ ○ ○
      61   62   63

2. Rehearsals that combine walk-throughs and camera rehearsal are most efficiently conducted from the (64) *studio floor* (65) *rehearsal hall* (66) *control room.*

   2 ○ ○ ○
      64   65   66

3. Camera rehearsal is conducted (67) *similarly to a dress rehearsal* (68) *for cameras only* (69) *for all technical operations but without talent.*

   3 ○ ○ ○
      67   68   69

4. If pressed for time, you should call for (70) *an uninterrupted camera rehearsal* (71) *a blocking rehearsal* (72) *a walk-through/camera rehearsal.*

   4 ○ ○ ○
      70   71   72

5. When engaged in EFP, you need not worry about (73) *talent and technical walk-throughs* (74) *cross-overs from one location to the next* (75) *the various camera positions.*

   5 ○ ○ ○
      73   74   75

SECTION TOTAL [ ]

Mark the following statements as true or false by filling in the bubbles in the *T* (for true) or *F* (for false) column.

	T	F
1	○ 76	○ 77
2	○ 78	○ 79
3	○ 80	○ 81
4	○ 82	○ 83
5	○ 84	○ 85
6	○ 86	○ 87
7	○ 88	○ 89
8	○ 90	○ 91
9	○ 92	○ 93
10	○ 94	○ 95

1. Because the director is engaged in artistic activities, knowledge of the technical production aspects is relatively unimportant.

2. Although the program objective is important to the director in the production phase, it is relatively unimportant in preproduction.

3. Proper visualization is essential for correct sequencing.

4. A good floor plan will greatly facilitate camera and talent blocking.

5. When marking a script, the ready cues must be written in just before the actual take cues.

6. If the script marking simply indicates "②" for the shot that is on the air and "③" for the next, it implies that you should give a "Ready three" cue and then call for a "Take three."

7. During a walk-through/camera rehearsal, the director rehearses primarily from the studio floor.

8. When doing an EFP, uninterrupted camera rehearsals are more important than when doing a studio show.

9. The "notes" activity during a production requires scheduled time for the corresponding "reset."

10. When directing a daily newscast, you do not need a floor plan to preplan the camera shots.

SECTION TOTAL [   ]

PROBLEM-SOLVING APPLICATIONS

1. When asked to direct an on-location television adaptation of the current theater arts department stage play in the local park, you are advised by the theater director of the play that he will determine the number and the positions of the cameras because he, after all, knows the stage blocking better than you do. What is your reaction? What would you suggest?

2. You are to determine on-camera shots and mark a script for an involved scene of a three-camera, live-on-tape situation comedy. The producer tells you that all she can give you is the script, not the complete floor plan. Because of a computer failure, the art director cannot transfer his rough sketch into a finished floor plan, and there is no way to get it to you before rehearsal. Can you proceed with your preproduction activities? If so, how? If not, why not?

3. When you're directing an EFP of a documentary segment on the lumber industry, the producer tells you not to worry too much about shot continuity because he intends to put the show together in extensive postproduction editing. Do you agree with the producer? If so, why? If not, why not?

4. During the evening news, the wrong story comes up on the server monitor. What can you do?

5. During an O/S sequence in a multicamera dramatic production, one of the actors has trouble hitting the blocking marks and is frequently obscured by the camera-near person. What advice would you give the actor?

Scale: 1/4" = 1'

Property List

Scale: 1/4" = 1'

Property List

Scale: 1/4" = 1'

Property List